BASEBALL
RULES
ILLUSTRATED

BASEBALL RULES ILLUSTRATED

Edited by George Sullivan

Produced by Charles Fellows

CORNERSTONE LIBRARY
Published by Simon & Schuster
NEW YORK

Published by Cornerstone Library, Inc.
A Simon & Schuster Division of
Gulf & Western Corporation
1230 Avenue of the Americas
New York, New York 10020

CORNERSTONE LIBRARY and colophon are
trademarks of Simon & Schuster, registered
in the U. S. Patent and Trademark Office.

Library of Congress Cataloging in Publication Data

Sullivan, George, 1927—
    Baseball rules illustrated.

    1. Baseball—Rules.   I. Title.
GV877.S94   796.357' 02' 022   80-27730

ISBN 0-346-12524-3

Manufactured in the
United States of America

10 9 8 7 6 5 4 3 2 1

INTRODUCTION

Dickey Pearce, a quick-witted shortstop with the Brooklyn Excelsiors in the 1850s, when baseball was just beginning, often schemed to beat the rules.

Dickey was the first to discover that by merely stopping the ball with the bat and nudging it down in front of the plate, he could easily speed to first base before any player could field the ball and throw him out. This form of batting—bunting, it came to be called—was often condemned, and some observers believed that bunting would eventually destroy baseball.

Dickey did more. He learned to place his bunts in such a way that the ball would bounce in fair territory and then roll foul across the third-base line, well out of the reach of either the third baseman or catcher. In those days, a batted ball was fair just as long as it landed fair.

While in the field, Dickey also plotted to outwit the rulebook. He would pretend to catch a ball, forcing the runner on first, afraid of being doubled up, to hold his base. Then Dickey would allow the ball to trickle through his hands to the ground, creating an easy force play at second base. Sometimes even a double play resulted.

Dickey's inventions tormented baseball for decades. But toward the end of the century any batted

7

ball that landed fair and then went foul was ruled a foul ball, and the trapped-ball trick fell victim to the infield-fly rule.

It is by means of such trial and error that the rules of baseball developed. The result is a lengthy and sophisticated set of rules, with myriad refinements.

But even to begin with, baseball was not a simple game. Just try explaining baseball to a friend who is unfamiliar with it. Even scoring a run, which means touching four bases in the proper sequence, is a complicated piece of business, for the conditions under which the bases may be touched include such concepts as balls and strikes, fair and foul territory, safe and out, and innings and the completion thereof. It takes several rulebook pages to explain how to score a run and there's an entire rulebook section devoted to putting the ball in play.

A quick glance at the rulebook would seem to indicate that every eventuality has been covered. Not true. Players in the tradition of Dickey Pearce never stop seeking to subvert things. For example, Rule 8.02, to combat the spitball, stated, "A pitcher shall not bring his pitching hand in contact with his mouth or lips while in the 18-foot circle surrounding the pitching rubber." Pitchers countered with the vaseline ball and the grease ball. So, beginning with the 1974 season, umpires were given complete authority for ruling on whether the

ball carries any "foreign substance," or whether the pitcher has any such substance on his person. Don't worry, pitchers will answer back.

The modern day player has his own way of looking at the rulebook. During the 1979 season, umpires Nick Bremigan and Don Denkinger went to pitcher Mike Marshall, then with the Twins, and Gene Mauch, the manager, to discuss Marshall's alleged practice of scuffing up baseballs. Marshall didn't want to talk to the umpires. "Put it in writing," he said, "and I'll give it to my lawyer." Dickey Pearce would have liked that.

1.00

OBJECTIVES OF THE GAME

Baseball is a game played between two teams of nine players, each under the direction of a manager. It is played on an enclosed field in accordance with these rules, and under the jurisdiction of one or more umpires (1.01).

The objective of each team is to win by scoring more runs than the opponent (1.02).

The winner of the game shall be that team which scores the greatest number of runs at the conclusion of a regulation game (1.03).

The Playing Field. The field shall be laid out according to the instructions below, supplemented by the diagrams on pages 10 and 11 (1.04).

The infield shall be a 90-foot square. The outfield shall be the area between the two foul lines formed by extending two sides of the square.

The distance from home base to the nearest fence, stand, or other obstruction on fair territory shall be 250 feet or more. A distance of 320 feet or more along the foul lines and 400 feet or more to center field is preferable.

The infield shall be graded so that the base lines and home plate are level. The pitcher's plate shall be 10 inches above the level of home plate. The degree of slope

9

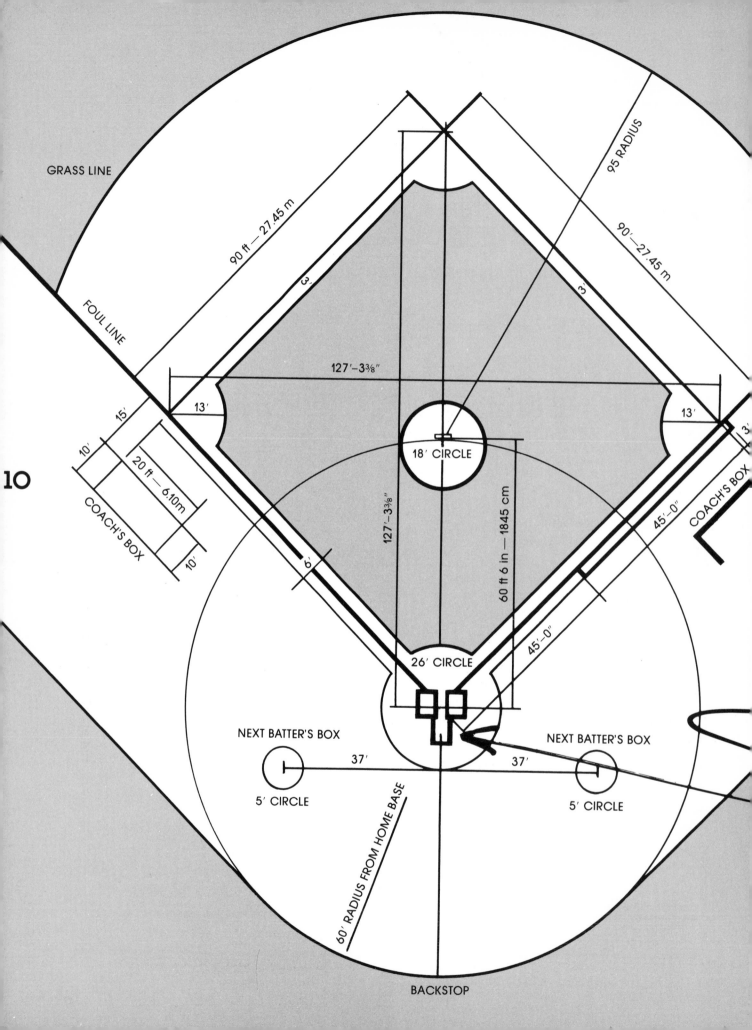

GRASS LINE

95 RADIUS

90 ft — 27.45 m

90'—27.45 m

FOUL LINE

3'

3'

127'-3³⁄₈"

13'

13'

15'

18' CIRCLE

3'

10'

20 ft — 6.10m

COACH'S BOX

COACH'S BOX

127'-3³⁄₈"

60 ft 6 in —1845 cm

45'-0"

10'

6'

45'-0"

26' CIRCLE

10

NEXT BATTER'S BOX

37'

37'

NEXT BATTER'S BOX

5' CIRCLE

60' RADIUS FROM HOME BASE

5' CIRCLE

BACKSTOP

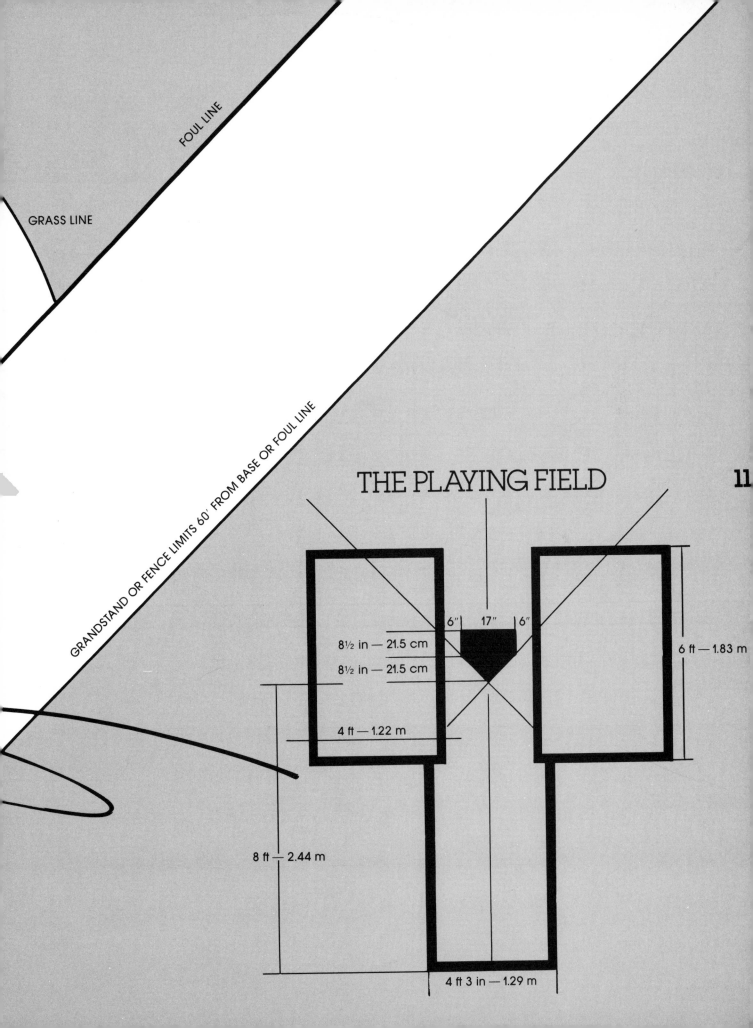

GRASS LINE

FOUL LINE

GRANDSTAND OR FENCE LIMITS 60' FROM BASE OR FOUL LINE

6" 17" 6"

8½ in — 21.5 cm

8½ in — 21.5 cm

6 ft — 1.83 m

4 ft — 1.22 m

8 ft — 2.44 m

4 ft 3 in — 1.29 m

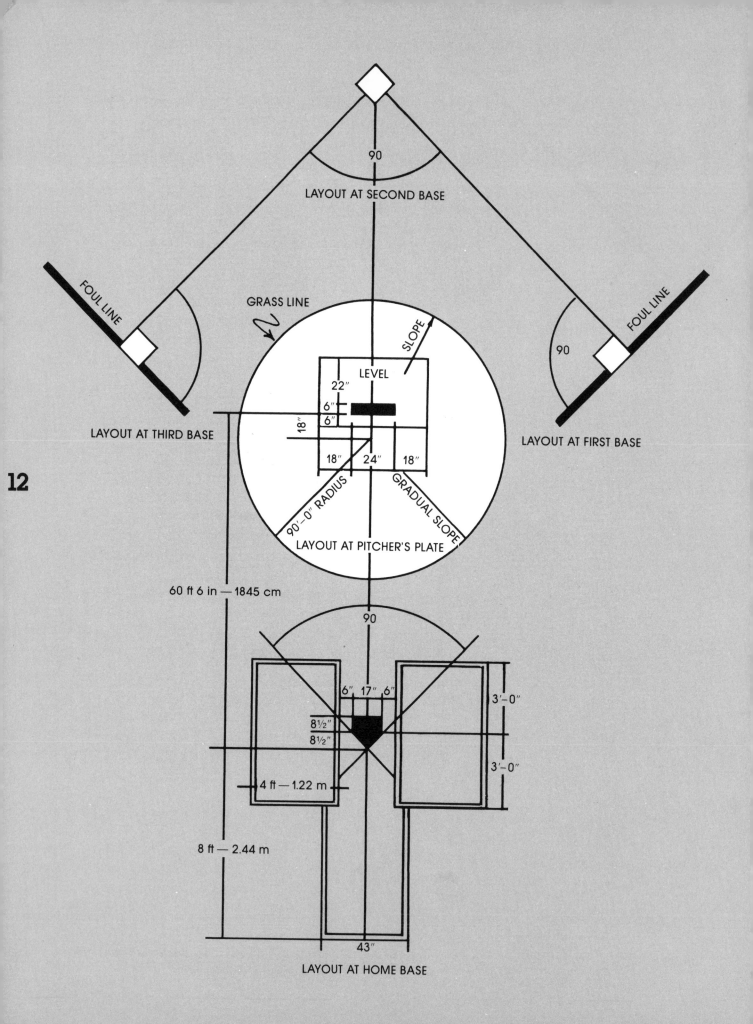

LAYOUT AT SECOND BASE

FOUL LINE

GRASS LINE

SLOPE

LEVEL

22"

6"

6"

18"

18" 24" 18"

FOUL LINE

90

LAYOUT AT THIRD BASE

LAYOUT AT FIRST BASE

90'-0" RADIUS

GRADUAL SLOPE

LAYOUT AT PITCHER'S PLATE

12

60 ft 6 in — 1845 cm

90

6" 17" 6"

3'-0"

8½"

8½"

3'-0"

4 ft — 1.22 m

8 ft — 2.44 m

43"

LAYOUT AT HOME BASE

from a point 6 inches in front of the pitcher's plate to a point 6 feet toward home plate shall be 1 inch to 1 foot, and the degree of slope is to be uniform.

The infield and outfield, including the boundary lines are considered to be fair territory. All other area is foul territory.

It is desirable that an imaginary line from home base through the pitcher's plate to second base shall run east-northeast.

It is recommended that the distance from home base to the backstop and from the baselines to the nearest fence, stand or other obstruction on foul territory shall be 60 feet or more.

Once the location of home base has been determined, to establish where second base is to be located, measure 127 feet, 3 3/8 inches in the desired direction, using a steel tape measure. From home base, measure 90 feet toward first base. From second base, measure 90 feet toward first base. The intersection of these lines establishes first base.

From home base, measure 90 feet toward third base. From second base, measure 90 feet toward third base. The intersection of these lines establishes third base.

The distance between first base and third base is 127 feet, 3 3/8 inches. All measurements from home base shall be taken from the point where the first and third base lines intersect.

The catcher's box, the batters' boxes, the coaches' boxes, the three-foot base lines and the next-batters' boxes shall be laid out as shown in the diagrams on pages 10 and 11.

The foul lines and all other playing lines indicated in the diagrams by means of solid black lines shall be marked with wet lime, chalk or other white material.

The grass lines and related dimensions shown on the diagrams are those used in many fields, but they are not mandatory. Each club shall determine the size and shape of the grassed and bare areas of its playing field.

● Any playing field constructed by a professional club after June 1, 1958, shall provide a minimum distance of 325 feet from home base to the nearest fence, stand or other obstruction on the right and left field foul lines, and a minimum distance of 400 feet to the center-field fence (a).

● No existing playing field shall be remodeled after June 1, 1958, in such a manner as to reduce the distance from home plate to the foul poles, and to the center-field fence, below the minimum specified in the paragraph above (b).

Home base shall be marked by a five-sided slab of whitened rubber. It shall be a 12-inch square with two of the corners filled in so that one edge is 17 inches long, two edges are 8 1/2 inches long, and two are 12 inches long. It shall be set in the ground with the point at the intersection of the lines extending from first base to home base, and from third base to home base. The 17-inch edge is facing the pitcher's plate and the two 12-inch edges are to coincide with the first and third base lines. The top edges of the home base are to be beveled, and the base shall be fixed in the ground level with the ground surface. See diagram on page 10 (1.05).

First, second and third bases shall be marked by white canvas bags, and securely attached to the ground, as indicated in the diagram on page 12. The first and third base bags shall be entirely within the infield. The second base bag shall be centered on second base. Each of the base bags shall be 15 inches, not less than 3 nor more than 5 inches thick, and filled with soft material (1.06).

The pitcher's plate shall be a rectangular slab of whitened rubber, 24 inches by 6 inches. It shall be set in the ground as shown in the diagrams on page 12, so that the distance between the pitcher's plate and home base (the rear point of home plate) shall be 60 feet, 6 inches (1.07).

The home club shall furnish players' benches, one for the home and one for the visiting teams. The benches are not to be less than 25 feet from the base lines. The benches are to be roofed and enclosed at the back and ends (1.08).

The ball is to be a sphere formed by yarn wound around a small core of cork, rubber or similar material, and covered with two strips of white horsehide or cowhide, tightly stitched together. It is to weigh not less than 5 nor more than 5 1/4 ounces avoirdupois, and measure not less than 9 nor more than 9 1/4 inches in circumference (1.09).

14

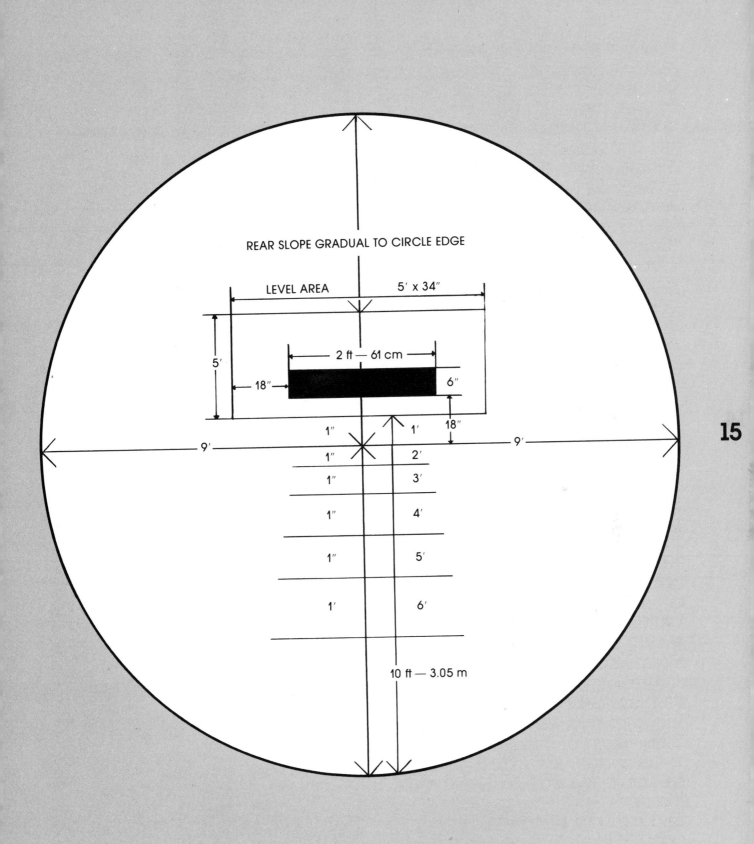

REAR SLOPE GRADUAL TO CIRCLE EDGE

LEVEL AREA   5' x 34"

2 ft — 61 cm

5'

18"   6"

                                    18"

1"   1'

9'   9'   **15**

1"   2'

1"   3'

1"   4'

1"   5'

1'   6'

10 ft — 3.05 m

THE PITCHING MOUND

The bat shall be a smooth, rounded stick, not more than 2 3/4 inches in diameter at the thickest part, and no more than 42 inches in length (1.10).

- The bat shall be (a):

(1) One piece of solid wood or

(2) Formed from a block of wood consisting of two or more pieces of wood bonded together with an adhesive in such a way that the grain direction of all pieces is essentially parallel to the length of the bat. Any laminated bat shall contain only wood or adhesive, except for a clear finish.

- The bat handle may be covered or treated with any material (including pine tar) to improve the grip, but such material cannot extend for more than 18 inches from the bat end. Any such material, including pine tar, which, in the umpire's judgment, extends beyond the 18-inch limitation, shall cause the bat to be removed from the game. No such material shall improve the reaction or distance factor of the bat (b).

- No colored bat may be used in a professional game unless approved by the rules committee (c).

- Cupped bats. An indentation on the end of the bat up to 1 inch is the depth permitted, but it can be no wider than 2 inches and no less than 1 inch in diameter. The indentation must be curved. No foreign substance may be added to it (d).

16

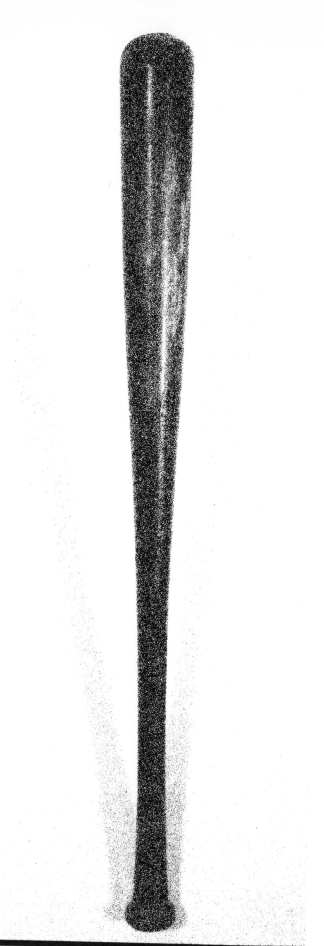

Uniforms (1.11).

● Color, trim and style (a).

(1) All players on a team shall wear uniforms that are identical in color, trim and style. All players' uniforms shall include minimal 6-inch numbers on their backs.

(2) Any part of an undershirt exposed to view shall be of a uniform standard color for all players on a team. Any player other than the pitcher may have numbers, letters and insignia attached to the sleeve of the undershirt.

(3) No player whose uniform does not conform to that of his teammates shall be permitted to participate in a game.

● A league may provide that (b):

(1) Each team shall wear a distinctive uniform at all times.

(2) Each team shall have two sets of uniforms, white for home games and a different color for road games.

● Sleeve lengths (c).

(1) Sleeves may vary for individual players, but the sleeves of each individual player shall be approximately the same length.

(2) No player shall wear ragged, frayed or slit sleeves.

● No player shall attach to his uniform any other material that is a different color from the uniform (d).

● No part of a uniform shall include a color pattern that imitates or suggests the shape of a baseball (e).

● Glass buttons and polished metal shall not be used on a uniform (f).

● No player shall attach anything to the heel or toes of his shoe other than the ordinary shoe plate or toe plate. Shoes with pointed spikes similar to golf or track shoes shall not be worn (g).

toe plate

catcher's protective gear

face mask

chest protector

shin guards

18

The catcher may wear a leather mitt not more than 38 inches in circumference, and not more than 15 1/2 inches from top to bottom. Such limits shall include all lacing and any leather band or facing attached to the other edge of the mitt.

The space between the thumb section and finger section of the mitt shall not exceed 6 inches at the top of the mitt and 4 inches at base of the thumb crotch.

The web shall measure not more than 7 inches across the top and not more than 6 inches from its top to the base of the thumb crotch. The web may be either a lacing, lacing through leather tunnels or a center-piece of leather, which may be an extension of the palm, connected to the mitt with lacing and constructed so that it will not exceed any of the above mentioned measurements (1.12).

catcher's mitt

The first baseman may wear a leather glove or mitt not more than 12 inches long from top to bottom, and not more than 8 inches wide across the palm, measured from the base of the thumb crotch to the outer edge of the mitt.

The space between the thumb section and the finger section of the mitt shall not exceed 4 inches at the top of the mitt and 3 1/2 inches at the base of the thumb crotch. The mitt shall be constructed so that this space is permanently fixed and cannot be enlarged, expanded, widened or deepened by the use of any materials or process.

The web of the mitt shall measure not more than 5 inches from its top to the base of the thumb crotch. The web may be either a lacing, lacing through leather tunnels or a center-piece of leather, which may be an extension of the palm, connected to the mitt with lacing and constructed so that it will not exceed the above-mentioned measurements.

The webbing shall not be constructed of wound or wrapped lacing, or deepened to make a net kind of trap. The glove may be of any weight (1.13).

first baseman's glove

Each fielder, other than the first baseman or catcher, may use or wear a leather glove. The measurements covering the size of the glove shall be made by measuring the front, or ball, receiving side of the glove.

The glove shall not measure more than 12 inches from the tip of any one of its four fingers, through the ball pocket, to the bottom edge, or heel of the glove.

The glove shall not measure more than 7 3/4 inches in width, as measured from the inside seam at the base of the first finger, along the base of the other fingers, to the outside edge of the little finger of the glove.

The space between the thumb and first finger, called the crotch, may be filled with leather webbing or a backstop.The webbing may be constructed of two plies of standard leather to close the crotch area entirely, or it may consist of a series of leather tunnels, leather panels or a lacing of leather thongs. The webbing may not be constructed of wound or wrapped lacing so as to make a net type of trap.

When the webbing is made to cover the entire crotch area, the webbing can be constructed so as to be flexible. When constructed of a series of sections, they must be joined together. These sections may not be constructed so as to permit a depression to be developed by curvatures in the section sides.

The webbing shall be made to control the size of the crotch opening. The crotch opening shall measure not more than 4 1/2 inches at the top, not more than 5 3/4 inches deep, and shall be 3 1/2 inches wide at its bottom. The opening of the crotch shall not be more than 4 1/2 inches at any point below its top. The webbing shall be secured at the top, bottom and sides of the crotch.

The crotch is to be attached with leather lacing. Should the crotch connections stretch or become loose, they shall be adjusted to the proper specifications. The glove can be of any weight (1.14).

Pitcher's Glove (1.15).
- The pitcher's glove shall be uniform in color, including all stitching, lacing and webbing. The pitcher's glove may not be white or gray (a).
- No pitcher shall attach to his glove any foreign material of a color different from his glove (b).

A professional league shall adopt the following rule pertaining to the use of helmets (1.16):
- All players shall use some type of protective helmet while at bat (a).
- All players in National Association Leagues, and those players in the major leagues who played with National Association clubs the previous year, shall wear ear-flap helmets while at bat. Players in the major leagues without pre-

vious professional experience are also included in this rule.

If an umpire observes a violation of these rules, he shall direct the violation to be corrected. If, in the umpire's judgment, the violation is not corrected within a reasonable time, the umpire shall eject the offender from the game (b).

Playing equipment, including, but not limited to, the bases, pitcher's plate, baseball bats, uniforms, catchers' mitts, first basemens' gloves, infielders' and outfielders' gloves, and protective helmets, as detailed in the provisions of this rule, shall not contain any undue commercialization of the product. Designations by the manufacturer on any such equipment must be in good taste as to the size and content of the manufacturer's logo or the brand name of the item. These provisions apply to professional leagues only (1.17).

fielder's glove

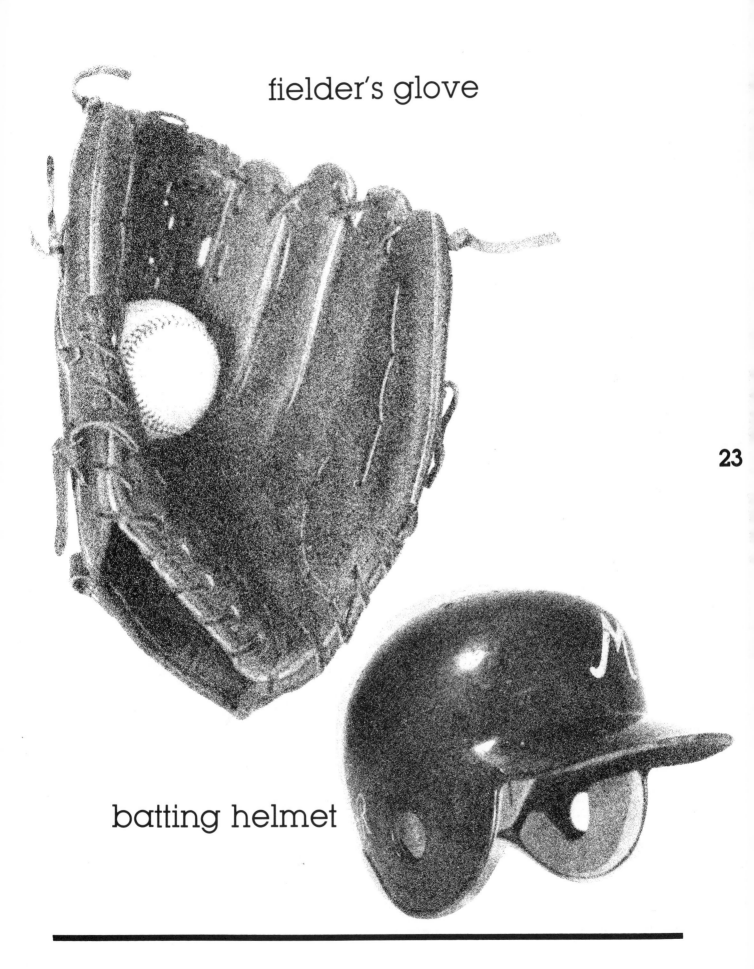

batting helmet

23

checked swing

(see page 94)

The manager or catcher
may request
the plate umpire
to ask his partner
for help
on a half swing when the
plate umpire calls the pitch a ball,
but not when the pitch is called a strike.

24

2.00

DEFINITIONS OF TERMS

adjudged A judgment decision by the umpire.

appeal The act of a fielder in claiming a breach of the rules by the offensive team.

balk An illegal act by the pitcher with a runner or runners on base, and which entitles all the runners to advance one base.

ball A pitch that does not enter the strike zone in flight and is not struck at by the batter.

base One of the four points that must be touched by a runner in order to score a run.

base coach A team member in uniform who is stationed in either the first or third base coach's box, and whose duty it is to direct the batter and base runners.

base on balls The award of first base to a batter who, during his time at bat, receives four pitches outside the strike zone.

batter An offensive player who takes his position in the batter's box.

batter-runner An offensive player who has just finished his time at bat and who has not been

25

put out, nor has the play in which he became a runner ended.

batter's box The area within which the batter stands during his time at bat.

battery The pitcher and the catcher.

bench The seating facilities reserved for the players, substitutes, and other team members in uniform when they are not actively engaged on the playing field. Also called dugout.

bunt A batted ball not swung at fully, but intentionally met with the ball and tapped slowly within the infield.

called game A game which, for any reason, is terminated by the umpire-in-chief.

catch The act of a fielder in getting secure possession of a ball in flight in his hand or glove, providing he does not use his cap, protector, pocket, or any part of his uniform in getting possession. It is not a catch, however, if simultaneously or immediately following his contact with the ball, he collides with a player, a wall, or falls down, and drops the ball as a result.

It is not a catch if a fielder touches a fly ball which then hits a member of the offensive team or an umpire, and then is caught by another defensive player.

If the fielder has made the catch and drops the ball while in the act of making a throw following the catch, the ball shall adjudged to have been caught.

In establishing the validity of the catch, the fielder shall hold the ball long enough to prove that he has complete control of it, and that his release of the ball is voluntary and intentional.

catcher The fielder who takes his position in back of the home base.

catcher's box The area within which the catcher stands until the pitcher delivers the ball.

club Person or group of persons responsible for assembling the team personnel, providing the playing field and required facilities, and representing the team in relations with the league.

batter squared around to bunt

coach   A team member in uniform appointed by the manager to perform such duties as the manager may designate, such as, but not limited to, acting as a base coach.

dead ball   A ball out of play because of a legally created suspension of play.

defensive team   The team in the field.

double-header   Two regularly scheduled games played in immediate succession.

double play   A play by the defense in which two offensive players are put out as a result of continuous action, providing there is no error between putouts.
•   A force double play is one in which both put outs are force plays (a).
•   A reverse force double play is one in which the first out is a force play, and the second out is made on a runner for whom the force is removed by reason of the first out (b).

dugout   See bench.

fair ball   A batted ball that settles in fair ground between home and first base, between home and third base, or that is in or over fair territory when bounding to the outfield past first or third base. A fair ball also occurs when a batted ball touches first, second or third base, or that falls in fair territory in or beyond first base or third base, or that, while in or over fair territory, touches an umpire or player, or that, while over fair territory, passes out of the playing field in flight.

A fair fly shall be judged according to the relative position of the ball and the foul line, including the foul pole, and not as to whether the fielder is in fair or foul territory at the time he touches the ball.

fair territory   That part of the playing field within and including the first base and third base lines extending from home base to the bottom of the playing field fences and upwards at right angles. All foul lines are in fair territory.

fielder   Any defensive player.

fielder's choice   The act of a fielder who handles a fair grounder and, instead of throwing to first base in an attempt to put out the batter-runner, throws to another base in an effort to put out the preceding runner.

The term is also used by scorers to account for the advance of the batter-runner who takes one or more extra bases when the fielder who handles his safe hit, attempts to put out the preceding runner. It is also used by scorers to account for the advance of a runner (other than by a stolen base or error) while a fielder is attempting to put out another runner, or the advance of a runner made solely because of a defensive team's indifference.

fly ball A ball that goes high in the air in flight.

force play A play in which a runner loses his right to occupy a base by reason of the batter becoming a runner.

forfeited game A game declared ended by the umpire-in-chief for a violation of the rules. The score is declared to be 9 to 0 in favor of the offended team.

foul ball A batted ball that settles in foul territory between home and first base, between home and third base, that bounds past first and third base in or over foul territory, that falls in foul territory beyond first or third base, or that, while in or over foul territory, touches the person of an umpire, player, or any object foreign to the natural ground.
    A foul fly shall be judged according to the relative position of the ball and the foul line, including the foul pole, and not as to whether the fielder is in foul or fair territory at the time he touches the ball.

foul territory That part of the playing field outside the first and third base lines as extended to the fences and extending upwards at right angles.

foul tip A batted ball that goes sharply and directly from the bat to the catcher's hands and is caught. Any foul tip that is caught is a strike and the ball is legally in play.

ground ball A batted ball that rolls along or bounces close to the ground.

home team The team on whose grounds the game is played. If the game is played on neutral grounds, the home team is designated by mutual agreement.

illegal pitch A pitch delivered to the batter when the pitcher does not have his pivot foot in contact with the pitcher's plate. A quick pitch can also be an illegal pitch.

illegally batted ball A ball hit by a batter who has one or both feet outside the batter's box.

infielder A fielder who occupies a position in the infield.

infield fly A fair fly ball, but not a line drive or attempted bunt, which can be caught by an infielder with ordinary effort, when first and second, or first, second and third bases are occupied, and before two players are out. (The pitcher, catcher, and any outfielder who stations himself in the infield are considered infielders for the purpose of this rule.)

When it seems apparent that a batted ball will be an infield fly, the umpire shall immediately declare, "Infield Fly," for the benefit of the runners. If the ball is near the baseline, the umpire shall declare, "Infield fly, if fair."

The ball is alive and runners may advance at the risk of the ball being caught. The runners may also retouch and advance after the ball is touched, the same as with any fly ball. If a hit becomes a foul ball, it is treated as a foul.

If a declared infield fly is allowed to fall untouched to the ground, and bounces foul before passing first or third base, it is a foul ball. If a declared infield fly falls untouched to the ground outside the base line, and bounces fair before passing first or third base, it is an infield fly.

in flight A batted, thrown or pitched ball which has not yet touched the ground or some object other than a fielder.

in jeopardy When a ball is in play and an offensive player is liable to be put out.

inning That portion of a game within which the teams alternate on offense and defense and in which there are three put-outs for each team. Each team's time at bat constitutes one half-inning.

interference The rules designate four different types of interference. In the case of each, the ball is declared dead.
● Offensive interference is an act by the team at bat that interferes with, obstructs, impedes, hinders, or confuses any fielder attempting to make a play. (If the umpire declares the batter, batter-runner, or runner to be out for interference, all other runners must return to the last base legally touched at the time of the interference, unless otherwise provided by the rules) (a).
● Defensive interference is an act by a fielder that hinders or prevents a batter from hitting a pitch (b).
● Umpire's interference occurs when an umpire hinders or impedes a catcher who is throwing in an attempt to prevent a stolen base. Umpire's interference also

occurs when a fair ball touches an umpire in fair territory before passing a fielder (c).
● Spectator interference occurs when a spectator reaches out of the stands, goes onto the playing field, or touches a live ball (d).

league A group of clubs whose teams play each other for the championship.

league president The officer designated to enforce the official rules, resolve any disputes involving the rules, and make judgments in the case of protested games. The league president may fine or suspend any player, coach, manager, or umpire for any violation of the rules.

legal In accordance with the rules.

line drive A batted ball that goes sharply and directly from the bat to a fielder without touching the ground.

live ball A ball that is in play.

manager The person appointed by the club to be responsible for a team's action on the field, and to represent the team in its relations with the umpire and opposing team. A player may be appointed manager.
● The club shall designate the manager to the league president or the umpire-in-chief not less

than 30 minutes before the scheduled starting time of the game (a).
● The manager may advise the umpire that he has delegated specific duties to a player or coach, but the manager shall be responsible for the team's conduct, observance of the official rules, and deference to the umpires (b).
● If the manager leaves the field, he must designate a player or coach as his substitute, and the substitute will then have the rights and responsibilities of the manager. If the manager fails to designate a substitute before his departure, the umpire-in-chief shall make the designation (c).

obstruction The act of a fielder who, while not in possession of the ball nor in the act of fielding it, impedes the progress of any runner.

offense The team at bat.

out One of the three required retirements of the offensive team during its time at bat.

outfielder A fielder who occupies a position in the outfield.

overslide An act by an offensive player when sliding into second, third or home base, in which his momentum is such that he loses contact with the base.

penalty   The application of the rules following an illegal act.

(the) person   Any part of a player's or umpire's body, clothing, or equipment.

pitch   A ball delivered to the batter by the pitcher.

pitcher   The fielder designated to deliver the pitch to the batter.

The pitcher's plate shall be a rectangular slab of whitened rubber, 24 inches by 6 inches. It shall be set in the ground as shown in the diagrams on page 12, so that the distance between the pitcher's plate and home base (the rear point of home plate) shall be 60 feet, 6 inches (1.07).

pivot foot   The pitcher's foot that is in contact with the pitcher's plate as he delivers the pitch.

"Play"   The umpire's order to start the game or to resume action following any dead ball situation.

quick return pitch   A pitch made with the intent of catching the batter off balance. A quick return pitch is an illegal pitch.

retouch   The act of a runner in returning to a base as legally required.

rubber   See pitcher's plate.

run   The Score made by an offensive player who touches first, second, third, and home bases in that order.

run down   An attempt by fielders to put out a runner between bases.

runner   An offensive player who is advancing toward, touching, or returning to base.

"Safe"   An umpire's declaration that a runner is entitled to the base for which he was trying.

set position   Along with the windup position, one of two legal pitching positions.

umpire calls time

swinging strike

squeeze play   The play that occurs when a team with a runner on third base attempts to score that runner by means of a bunt.

strike   A legal pitch, so called by the umpire, that:
- Is struck at by the batter and missed (a).
- Is not struck at, but passes through any part of the strike zone (b).
- Is fouled by the batter when the count is less than two strikes (c).
- Is bunted foul (d).
- Touches the batter as he strikes at it (e).
- Touches the batter in flight in the strike zone (f).
- Is a foul tip (g).

strike zone   The space over home plate which is between the batter's armpits and the top of his knees when he assumes his natural stance. The umpire determines the strike zone according to the batter's usual stance when he swings at a pitch.

suspended game   A terminated game that is to be completed at a later date.

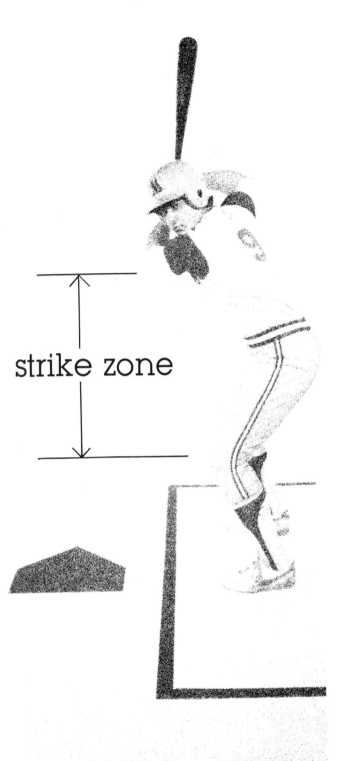

strike zone

tag   The action of a fielder in touching a base with his body while holding the ball securely in his hand or glove. A tag can also refer to the action of a fielder in touching a runner with the ball, or with his hand or glove while securely holding the ball in his hand or glove.

throw   The act of propelling the ball with the arm and hand, as distinct from the pitch.

tie game   A regulation game that is called when each team has the same number of runs.

"Time"   The announcement by an umpire of a legal interruption of play. The ball is declared dead when "Time!" is called.

triple play   A play by the defense in which three offensive players are put out as a result of continuous action, providing there is no error between putouts.

wild pitch   A pitch that is so high, low, or wide of the plate that it cannot be handled by the catcher with ordinary effort.

wind-up position   Along with the set position, one of the two legal pitching positions.

catcher blocks
plate

wild pitch

3.00 GAME PRELIMINARIES

Before the game, the umpire shall (3.01):

● Require the strict observance of all rules governing the implements of play and equipment of the players (a).

● Be sure that all playing lines are marked with lime, chalk, or other white material easily distinguishable from the ground or grass (b).

● Receive from the home club a supply of regulation baseballs, the number and make to be certified to the home club by the league president. Each ball shall be enclosed in a sealed package bearing the signature of the league president. The seal is not to be broken until just prior to game time when the umpire shall open each package to inspect the ball and remove its gloss. The umpire shall be the sole judge of the fitness of the balls to be used in the game (c).

● Be assured by the home club that at least one dozen regulation reserve balls are immediately available for use if required (d).

● Have in his possession at least two alternate balls. The umpire shall require the replenishment of the supply of alternate balls as needed throughout the game (e).

The alternate balls shall be put in play when:

(1) A ball has been batted out of the playing field into the spec-

39

tator area.

(2) A ball has become discolored or otherwise rendered unfit for further use.

(3) A pitcher requests an alternate ball.

The umpire shall not give an alternate ball to the pitcher until play has ended and the previously used ball is declared dead. After a thrown or batted ball goes out of the playing field, play shall not be resumed with an alternate ball until the runners have reached the bases to which they are entitled. After a home run is hit out of the playing grounds, the umpire shall not deliver a new ball to the pitcher or the catcher until the batter hitting the home run has crossed home plate.

No player shall intentionally discolor or damage the ball by rubbing it with soil, rosin, paraffin, licorice, sand paper, emery paper, or other foreign substance. In such cases, the umpire shall demand the ball and remove the offender from the game. In case the umpire cannot locate the offender, and should the pitcher deliver a discolored or damaged ball to the batter, the pitcher shall be removed from the game at once and shall be automatically suspended for ten days (3.02).

A player or players may be substituted for during a game any time the ball is dead. A substitute player shall bat in the replaced player's position in the batting order. A player once

removed from a game is not permitted to re-enter the game (3.03).

If a substitute enters the game in place of a player-manager, the manager may thereafter go to the coaching lines at his discretion.

When two or more substitute players of the defensive enter the game at the same time, the manager shall, immediately before they take their positions as fielders, designate to the umpire-in-chief such players' positions in the team's batting order. The umpire-in-chief shall then so notify the official scorer. If this information is not immediately given to the umpire-in-chief, he shall have the authority to designate the substitutes' places in the batting order (3.03).

A pitcher may change to another position only once during the same inning. In other words, the pitcher will not be allowed to assume a position other than a pitcher more than once during the same inning.

Any player other than a pitcher that is substituted for an injured player shall be allowed five warm-up throws.

Any player whose name is on his team's batting order may not become a substitute runner for another member of his team. This rule is intended to eliminate the practice of using a so-called courtesy runner for a teammate. No player who has been in the

game and has been taken out for a substitute shall return as a courtesy runner. Any player not in the lineup shall be considered a substitute player, if used as a courtesy runner (3.04).

The pitcher named in the batting order that is handed to the umpire-in-chief (as provided in rules 4.01 and 4.01 b) shall pitch to the first batter or any substitute batter until such batter is put out or reaches first base, unless the pitcher sustains an injury or becomes ill, which, in the judgment of the umpire-in-chief, incapacitates him from pitching (3.05)(a).

If the pitcher is replaced, the substitute pitcher shall pitch to the batter then at bat or any substitute batter, until such batter is put out or reaches first base, or until the offensive team is put out, unless the substitute pitcher sustains an injury or becomes ill and, in the judgment of the umpire-in-chief, is thereby incapacitated from further play as a pitcher (b).

If an improper substitution is made for the pitcher, the umpire shall direct the proper pitcher to return to the game until the provisions of this rule are fulfilled. If the improper pitcher is permitted to pitch, any play that results is legal. The improper pitcher becomes the proper pitcher as soon as he makes his first pitch to the batter, or as soon as any runner is put out. If a manager attempts to remove a pitcher in violation of this rule, the umpire is to notify him that it cannot be done. If, through oversight, the umpire-in-chief has announced the improper incoming pitcher, he should correct the situation before the improper pitcher pitches. Once the improper pitcher delivers a pitch, he becomes the proper pitcher (c).

The manager shall immediately notify the umpire-in-chief of any substitution, and shall state to the umpire-in-chief the substitute's place in his batting order. Players for whom substitutions have been made may remain with their team on the bench and may warm up pitchers. If a manager substitutes another player for himself, he may continue to direct his team from the bench or the coach's box. Umpires should not permit players for whom substitutions have been made, and who have remained on the bench, to address any remarks to any opposing player, manager, or the umpires (3.06).

The umpire-in-chief, after having been informed or notified of a substitution, shall immediately announce or cause to be announced each substitution (3.07).

If no announcement of a substitution is made, the substitute shall be considered as having entered the game when (3.08) (a):
(1) If a pitcher, he takes his place on the pitcher's plate.
(2) If a batter, he takes his place in the batter's box.
(3) If a fielder, he reaches the position usually occupied by the fielder he has replaced, and play commences.
(4) If a runner, he takes the place of the runner he has replaced.
● Any play made by or on any of the above mentioned unannounced substitutes shall be legal (b).

Players in uniform shall not address or mingle with spectators or sit in the stands before, during or after a game. No manager, coach or player shall address any spectator before or during a game. Players of opposing teams are not to fraternize at any time while in uniform (3.09).

The manager of the home team shall be the sole judge as to whether a game shall be started because of unsuitable weather conditions or the unfit condition of the playing field, except for the second game of a doubleheader. Any league, however, may authorize its president to suspend the application of this rule during the closing weeks of its championship season in order to assure that the championship is decided on its merits. When the postponement of and the possible failure to play a game between two teams in the final series of a championship season might affect the final standing of any club in the league, the president, on appeal from any club in the league, may assume the authority granted the home team manager by this rule (a).

● The umpire-in-chief of the first game of a double-header shall be the sole judge as to whether the second game of a double-header shall be started because of unsuitable weather conditions or the unfit condition of the playing field (b).

● The umpire-in-chief shall be the sole judge as to whether and when play shall be suspended during a game because of unsuitable weather conditions or the unfit condition of the playing field; as to whether or when play shall be resumed after such suspension. He shall not call the game until at least thirty minutes after he has suspended play. He may continue the suspension for as long as he believes there is any chance to resume play.

The umpire-in-chief shall at all times try to complete a game. His authority to resume play following one or more suspensions of as much as thirty minutes each shall be absolute and he shall terminate a game only when there appears no possibility of completing it (c).

Between games of a double-header, or whenever a game is suspended because of the unfitness of the playing field, the umpire-in-chief shall have control of groundkeepers and assistants for the purpose of making the playing field fit for play. When this rule is violated, the umpire-in-chief may forfeit the game to the visiting team (3.11).

When the umpire suspends play, he shall call "Time." The suspension is lifted and play resumes at the umpire's call of "Play." Between the call of "Time" and the call of "Play", the ball is dead (3.12).

43

TIME

The manager of the home team shall present to the umpire-in-chief and the opposing manager any ground rules that he thinks are necessary covering the overflow of spectators upon the playing field, batted or thrown balls in such overflow, or any other contingencies. If these rules are acceptable to the opposing manager, they shall be legal. If these rules are unacceptable to the opposing manager, the umpire-in-chief shall make and enforce any special ground rules he thinks are made necessary by ground conditions, but these rules are not to conflict with the official playing rules (3.13).

Members of the offensive team shall carry all gloves and other equipment off the field and dugout while the team is at bat. No equipment shall be left lying on the field, either in fair or foul territory (3.14).

No person shall be allowed on the playing field during a game except players and coaches in uniform, managers, news photographers authorized by the home team, umpires, officers of the law in uniform and watchmen or other employees of the home club. In the case of unintentional interference with play by any person herein authorized to be on the playing field, except umpires, the ball is alive and in play. If the interference is intentional, the ball shall be dead at the moment of the interference, and the umpire shall impose such penalties as in his opinion will nullify the act of interference.

The question of intentional or unintentional interference shall be decided on the basis of the person's action. For example, a bat boy, ball attendant, or policeman who tries to avoid being touched by a thrown or batted ball, but is still touched, would be involved in unintentional interference. If, however, he kicks the ball, picks it up or pushes it, that is considered intentional interference, regardless of what his thought might have been (3.15).

When there is spectator interference with any thrown or batted ball, the ball shall be dead at the moment of interference, and the umpire shall impose such penalties as in his opinion will nullify the act of interference. If spectator interference clearly prevents a fielder from catching a fly ball, the umpire shall declare the batter out.

There is a difference between a ball being thrown or batted into the stands, touching a spectator, and thereby being declared out of play (even though it rebounds out onto the field), and a spectator going out onto the field, or reaching over, under or through a barrier and touching a ball in play, or touching or otherwise interfering with a player. In the latter case, it is clearly intentional and should be dealt with as intentional interference (Rule 3.15). The batter and runners shall be placed where, in the umpire's judgment, they would have been, had the interference not occurred.

No interference shall be allowed when a fielder reaches over a fence, railing, rope or into a stand to catch a ball. He does so at his own risk. However, should a spectator reach out on the playing field side of such fence, railing or rope and plainly prevent the fielder from catching the ball, then the batsman should be called out for spectator's interference (3.16).

Players and substitutes of both teams shall confine themselves to their team's benches unless actually participating in the play, preparing to enter the game, or coaching at first or third base. No one except the players, substitutes, managers, coaches, trainers and bat boys shall occupy a bench during a game. For violation of this rule, the umpire may, after first issuing a warning, remove the offender from the field.

Players on the disabled list are permitted to participate in pre-game activity and sit on the bench during the game, but may not take part in any activity during the game, such as warming up a pitcher, bench-jockeying, etc. Disabled players are not

allowed to enter the playing surface at any time or for any purpose during the game (3.17).

The home team shall provide police protection sufficient to preserve order. If a person or persons enter the playing field during a game and interfere in any way with the play, the visiting team may refuse to play until the field is cleared. If the field is not cleared in a reasonable length of time, which in no case shall be less than fifteen minutes after the visiting team's refusal to play, the umpire may forfeit the game to the visiting team (3.18).

safe!

4.00

STARTING AND ENDING A GAME

STARTING AND ENDING A GAME—4.00

The **umpire**, or umpires, shall enter the playing field five minutes before the hour set for the game to begin, and proceed directly to the home base where they are to be met by the managers of the opposing teams (unless the home club has given previous notice that the game has been postponed or is to be delayed in starting) (4.01).

In sequence, this is what is to transpire:

● First, the home manager is to give his batting order, in duplicate, to the umpire-in-chief (a).

● Next, the visiting manager is to give his batting order, in duplicate, to the umpire-in-chief (b).

● The umpire-in-chief is to make certain that the original and copies of the respective batting orders are identical, and then tender a copy of each batting order to the opposing manager. The copy retained by the umpire shall be the official batting order. The tender of the batting order by the umpire shall establish the batting orders. Thereafter, no substitutions shall be made by either manager, except as provided in these rules (c).

● As soon as the home team's batting order is handed to the umpire-in-chief, the umpires are in charge of the playing field, and from that moment they shall have sole authority to determine when a game shall be called, suspended or resumed on account of the weather or the condition of the playing field.

Obvious errors in the batting order which are noticed by the umpire-in-chief before he calls, "Play", for the start of the game, should be called to the attention of the manager or captain of the team in error, so the necessary correction can be made before the game starts. For example, if a manager has inadvertently listed only eight men in the batting order, or has listed two players with the same last name but without any identifying initial, and the errors are noticed by the umpire before he calls, "Play", he shall cause such errors to be corrected. Teams should not be "trapped" later by some mistake that obviously was inadvertent and which can be corrected before the game starts (d).

The players of the home team shall take their defensive positions, the first batter of the visiting team shall take his position in the batter's box, the umpire shall call, "Play", and the game shall start (4.02).

When the ball is put in play at the start of or during a game, all fielders, other than the catcher, are to be in fair territory (4.03).

● The catcher shall station himself directly in back of the plate. He may leave his position at any time to catch a pitch or make a play. An exception occurs when the batter is being given an intentional base on balls, in which case the catcher must stand with both feet within the lines of the catcher's box until the ball leaves the pitcher's hand. The penalty for violating this rule is a balk called upon the pitcher (a).

● The pitcher, while in the act of delivering the ball to the batter, shall take his legal position (b).

● Except for the pitcher and the catcher, any fielder may station himself anywhere in fair territory (c).

● Except for the batter or a runner attempting to score, no offensive player shall cross the catcher's lines when the ball is in play (d).

The batting order shall be followed throughout the game, unless one player is substituted for another. In such a case, the substitute shall take the place of the replaced player in the batting order (4.04).

The offensive team shall station two base coaches on the field during its term at bat, one near first base and one near third base (4.05) (a).

● Base coaches shall be limited to two in number, shall be in team uniform, and remain within the coach's box at all time. For violating this rule, the offending coach shall be removed from the game and made to leave the playing field.

It has been common practice for many years for some coaches to put one foot outside the coach's box, stand astride or be slightly outside the lines that form the box. In such cases, the coach is not to be considered out of the box unless the opposition manager complains. The umpire shall then strictly enforce the rule and require all coaches on both teams to remain in the coach's box at all times.

It is also common practice for a coach who has a play at his base to leave the coach's box to signal the player to slide, advance or return to a base. This may be allowed if the coach does not interfere with the play in any manner (b).

No manager, player, substitute, coach, trainer or batboy, whether from the bench, the coach's box, the playing field or elsewhere, shall at any time (4.06) (a):

(1) Incite or try to incite a demonstration by spectators by either a word or sign.

(2) Use language which in any manner refers or reflects upon opposing players, an umpire or any spectator.

(3) Call "Time", or employ any other word or phrase or commit any act while the ball is alive or in play for the purpose of trying to make the pitcher commit a balk.

(4) Make intentional contact with the umpire in any manner.

● No fielder shall take a position in the batter's line of vision and, with deliberate unsportsmanlike conduct or intent, act in a manner to distract the batter. For violating this rule, the offender is to be removed from the game and is to leave the playing field. If a balk was made, it is to be nullified (b).

When a manager, player, coach or trainer is ejected from a game, he shall leave the field immediately and take no further part in the game. He is to remain in the clubhouse, or change to street clothes and then either leave the park or take a seat in the grandstand well-removed from the vicinity of the team's bench or bullpen. A manager, coach or player under suspension is not permitted in the dugout or pressbox during the course of a game (4.07).

When the occupants of a player's bench show violent disapproval of an umpire's decision, the umpire shall first give warn-ing that such disapproval shall cease. If such action continues, the umpire shall order the offenders from the bench to the clubhouse. If he is unable to detect the offender or offenders, he may clear the bench of all substitute players. The manager of the offending team shall have the privilege of recalling to the playing field only those players needed for substitution in the game (4.08).

How a team scores (4.09):
● One run is to be scored each time a runner legally advances to and touches first, second, third and home base before three men are put out to end the inning (a). An exception occurs and a run is

not to be scored if the runner advances to home base during a play in which the third out is made:

(1) By the batter-runner before he touches first base.
(2) By any runner being forced out.
(3) By a preceding runner who is declared out because he failed to touch one of the bases.

● When the winning run is scored in the last half-inning of a regulation game, or in the last half of an extra inning, as the result of a base on balls, hit batter, or any other play with the bases full which forces the runner on third to advance, the umpire is not to declare the game ended until the runner forced to advance from third base has touched home base and the batter-runner has touched first base. An exception can occur in cases where fans rush onto the field and physically prevent the runner from touching home plate, or the batter from touching first base. In such cases, the umpire shall award the runner the base because of the obstruction of the fans.

If the runner on third refuses to advance and touch home base in a reasonable amount of time, the umpire shall disallow the run, call the offending player out and order the game resumed. With two out, the batter-runner refuses to advance to and touch first base, the umpire shall disallow the run, call the offending player out, and order the game resumed. If, before two are out, the batter-runner refuses to advance and touch first base, the run shall count, but the offending player shall be called out (b).

A regulation game consists of nine innings, unless extended because of a tie score, or shortened because the home team needs none of its half of the ninth inning or only a fraction of it, or because the umpire calls the game (4.10) (a).

● If the score is tied after nine completed innings, play is to continue until (1) the visiting team has scored more total runs than the home team at the end of a completed inning, or (2) the home team scores the winning run in an uncompleted inning (b).

● If a game is called, it is a regulation game if (c):

(1) Five innings have been completed.
(2) The home team has scored more runs in four or four and a fraction half innings than the visiting team has scored in five completed half innings.
(3) The home team scores one or more runs in its half of the fifth inning to tie the score.

● If each team has the same number of runs when the game ends, the umpire shall declare a "tie game" (d).

● If a game is called before it has become a regulation game, the umpire shall declare "no game" (e).

The score of a regulation game is the total number of runs scored by each team at the moment the game ends (4.11).

● The game ends when the visiting team completes its half of the ninth inning, if the home team is ahead (a).

● The game ends when the ninth inning is completed, if the visiting team is ahead (b).

● If the home team scores the winning run in its half of the ninth inning (or its half of an extra inning after a tie), the game ends immediately when the winning run is scored. An exception occurs when the last batter in a game hits a home run out of the playing field, and the batter-runner and all runners on base are permitted to score in accordance with the base-running rules. The game ends when the batter-runner touches home plate.

Should a batter hit a home run out of the playing field to win the game in the last of the ninth inning or in an extra inning, but is called out for passing a preceding runner, the game ends immediately when the winning run is scored (c).

● A called game ends at the moment the umpire terminates play. An exception occurs if the game is called while any inning is in progress and before it is completed. The game then becomes a suspended game in each of the following situations (d):

(1) The visiting team has scored one or more runs to tie the score and the home team has not scored.

(2) The visiting team has scored one or more runs to take the lead and the home team has not tied the score or retaken the lead.

Suspended Games (4.12)

● A league shall adopt the following rules providing for the completion at a future date of games terminated for any of the following reasons (a):

(1) A curfew imposed by law.

(2) A time limit permissable under league rules.

(3) Light failure or malfunction of a mechanical field device under the control of the home club, such as an automatic tarpaulin or water removal equipment.

(4) Darkness, when a law prevents the lights from being turned on.

(5) Weather, if the game is called while an inning is in progress and before it is completed for one of the following reasons:

○ The visiting team has scored one or more runs to tie the score, and the home team has not scored (i).

○ The visiting team has scored one or more runs to take the lead, and the home team has not tied the score or taken the lead (ii).

● Such games will be known as suspended games. No game called because of a curfew, weather or time limit shall be deemed a suspended game unless it has progressed far enough to have been a regulation game under the provisions of Rule 4.10. A game called under the provisions of Rule 4.12 a (3) or (4) shall be deemed a suspended game at any time after it starts.

Weather and similar conditions —Rule 4.12 a (through 5)—shall take precedence in determining whether a called game shall be a suspended game. A game can only be considered a suspended game if stopped for any of the five reasons specified in Rule 4.12 a.

Any legal game called because of weather with the score tied (unless the situation outlined in Rule 4.12 a (5) (i) prevails) is a tie game and must be replayed in its entirety (4.12 b).

A suspended game shall be resumed and completed as follows (4.12 c):

(1) Immediately preceding the next scheduled single game between the two clubs on the same grounds.

(2) Immediately preceding the next scheduled double-header between the two clubs on the same grounds, if no single game remains on the schedule.

(3) If suspended on the last scheduled date between the two clubs in that city, transferred and played on the grounds of the opposing club, if possible:

○ Immediately preceding the next scheduled single game (i).

○ Immediately preceding the next scheduled doubleheader, if no single game remains on the schedule (ii).

(4) If a suspended game has not been resumed and completed on the last date scheduled for the two clubs, it shall be a called game.

● A suspended game shall be resumed at the exact point of suspension of the original game. The completion of a suspended game is a continuation of the original game.

The line-up and batting order of both teams shall be exactly the same as the line-ups and batting orders at the moment of suspension, subject to rules governing substitution. Any player may be replaced by a player who had not been in the game prior to the suspension. No player removed before the suspension may be returned to the line-up.

A player who was not with the club when the game was suspended is not to be used as a substitute, even if he has taken the place of a player no longer with the club who would not have been eligible because he

53

had been removed from the line-up before the game was suspended.

If immediately prior to the call of a suspended game a substitute pitcher has been announced, but he has not retired the side or pitched until the batter becomes a base runner, such a pitcher is not required to start the suspended game when it is resumed. However, if he does not start, he is to be considered as having been substituted for, and may not be used in the balance of the game (d).

Rules Governing Double-headers (4.13)

- Only two championship games are to be played on any one date. Completion of a suspended game shall not violate this rule (a) (1).

If two games are scheduled to be played for one admission on one date, the first game shall be the regularly scheduled game for that date (a) (2).

- After the start of the first game of a double-header, that game shall be completed before the second game of the double-header shall begin (b).

- The second game of a double-header shall start twenty minutes after the first game is completed, unless a longer interval—not to exceed thirty minutes—is declared by the umpire-in-chief and announced to the opposing managers at the end of the first game. An exception can occur if the league president has approved a request of the home club for a longer interval between games for some special event. In such a case, the umpire-in-chief shall declare the longer interval and announce it to the opposing managers. The umpire-in-chief of the first game shall be the timekeeper controlling the interval between games (c).

- If at all possible, the umpire shall start the second game of a double-header and play shall continue for as long as ground conditions, local time restrictions, or weather permit (d).

- When a regularly scheduled double-header is delayed starting for any cause, any game that is started is to be regarded as the first game of the double-header (e).

- When a rescheduled game is part of a double-header, the rescheduled game shall be regarded as the second game of the double-header, and the first game shall be then regarded as the regularly scheduled game for that date (f).

The umpire-in-chief shall order the playing field lights turned on whenever in his opinion darkness makes further play in daylight hazardous (4.14).

A game may be forfeited to the opposing team when a team (4.15):

- Fails to appear upon the field or, being upon the field, refuses to start play within five minutes after the umpire has called, "Play", at the appointed hour for beginning the game, unless such delayed appearance is, in the umpire's judgment, unavoidable (a).
- Employs tactics palpably designed to delay or shorten the game (b).
- Refuses to continue play during a game, unless the game has been suspended or terminated by the umpire (c).
- After a suspension of play, refuses to resume play within one minute after the umpire has called, "Play"(d)
- After a warning by the umpire, the team willfully and persistently violates any rules of the game (e).
- Fails to obey the umpire's order for the removal of player from the game within a reasonable time (f).
- Fails to appear for the second game of a double-header within twenty minutes after the close of the first game, unless the umpire-in-chief of the first game shall have extended the time of the intermission (g).

A game shall be forfeited to the visiting team if, after play has been suspended, the orders of the umpire to the groundkeepers regarding preparation of the field for the resumption of play are not complied with (4.16).

A game shall be forfeited to the opposing team when a team is unable or refuses to place nine players on the field (4.17).

If the umpire declares a game forfeited, he shall transmit a written report to the league president within twenty-four hours thereafter, but failure of such transmittal shall not affect the forfeiture (4.18).

Protesting Games. Each league shall adopt rules governing the procedure for protesting a game when a manager claims that an umpire's decision is in violation of these rules. No protest shall ever be permitted on a judgment decision of the umpire's. In all protested games, the decision of the league president shall be final.

Whenever a manager protests a game because of alleged misapplication of the rules, the protest will not be recognized unless the umpires are notified at the same time that the play under protest occurs, and before the next pitch is made or a runner is retired. A protest arising on a game-ending play may be filed until noon the following day with the league office (4.19).

umpire calls play

5.00

PUTTING THE BALL IN PLAY

PUTTING THE BALL IN PLAY: LIVE BALL—5.00

At the time set for beginning the game, the umpire shall call "Play" (5.01).

After the umpire calls "Play", the ball is alive and in play and remains alive and in play until, for legal cause, it becomes dead, or the umpire calls, "Time", suspending play. While the ball is dead, no player may be put out, no bases may be run and no runs may be scored, except that runners may advance one or more bases as the result of acts which occurred while the ball was alive, such as, but not limited to a balk, an overthrow, interference, a home run or other fair hit out of the playing field.

Should a ball come partially apart in a game, it is in play until the play is completed (5.02).

The pitcher shall deliver the pitch to the batter, who may elect to strike the ball or may not offer at it, as he chooses (5.03).

The offensive team's objective is to have its batter become a runner and its runners advance (5.04).

The defensive team's objective is to prevent offensive players from becoming runners, and to prevent their advance around the bases (5.05).

57

When a batter becomes a runner and touches all bases legally, he shall score one run for his team. A run legally scored cannot be nullified by subsequent action of the runner, such as, but not limited to, an effort to return to third base in the belief that he had left the base before a caught fly ball (5.06).

When three offensive players are put out, that team takes the field and the opposing team becomes the offensive team (5.07).

If a thrown ball accidentally touches a base coach, or a pitched or thrown ball touches an umpire, the ball is alive and in play. However, if the coach interferes with a thrown ball, the runner is out (5.08).

The ball becomes dead and the runners advance one base, or return to their bases without any liability of being put out, when (5.09):

- A pitched ball touches a batter or his clothing while he is in his legal batting position. The runners, if forced, advance (a).
- The plate umpire interferes with the catcher's throw; the runners may not advance. If the catcher's throw happens to retire the runner, the interference shall be disregarded (b).
- A balk is committed; runners advance (c).
- A ball is illegally batted; runners return (d).
- A foul ball is not caught; runners return. The umpire is not to put the ball in play until all runners have retouched their bases (e).
- A fair ball touches a runner or an umpire in fair territory before it touches an infielder, including the pitcher, or touches an umpire before it has passed an infielder other than the pitcher (f).

If a fair ball touches an umpire who is working in the infield after it has bounded past or over the pitcher, it is a dead ball. If a batted ball is deflected by a fielder in fair territory and hits a runner or an umpire while still in flight and then is caught by an infielder, it shall not be a catch, but the ball shall remain in play.

If a fair ball goes through or by an infielder and touches a runner immediately in back of him, or touches a runner after being deflected by an infielder, the ball is in play and the umpire shall not declare the runner out. In making such a decision, the umpire must be convinced that the ball passed through or by the infielder, and that no other infielder had a chance to make a play on the ball. In such cases, runners advance, if forced.

• A pitched ball passes the catcher and lodges in the umpire's mask or other paraphernalia. The runners advance (g).

If a foul tip hits the umpire and is caught by a fielder on the rebound, the ball is dead and the batter cannot be called out. The same applies in cases where the foul tip lodges in the umpire's mask or other paraphernalia.

If a third strike—not a foul tip—passes the catcher and hits an umpire, the ball is in play. If such a ball rebounds and is caught by a fielder before it touches the ground, the batter is not out on such a catch. The ball is to be considered in play and the batter may be retired at first base or touched with the ball for the out.

If a pitched ball passes the catcher and lodges in the umpire's mask or other paraphernalia on the third strike or fourth ball, then the batter is entitled to first base and all runners advance one base. If the count on the batter is less than three balls, the runners advance.

A ball lodging in the catcher's mask, protector or uniform is a live ball and in play.

• Any legal pitch touches a runner trying to score; runners advance (h).

The ball becomes dead when an umpire calls "Time." The umpire-in-chief shall call "Time" when (5.10):

• In his judgment, weather, darkness or similar conditions make further play impossible (a).

• When light failure makes it difficult or impossible for the umpires to follow play. (A league may adopt its own regulations governing games interrupted by light failure) (b).

• When an accident incapacitates a player or an umpire (c).

(1) If an accident to a runner is such as to prevent him from proceeding to a base to which he is entitled, as on a home run hit out of the playing field, or in the case of an award of one or more bases, a substitute runner shall be permitted to complete the play.

• When a manager requests "Time" for a substitution or for a conference with one of his players (d).

• When the umpire wishes to examine the ball, consult with either manager, or for any similar causes (e).

• When a fielder, after catching a fly ball, falls into a bench or stand, or falls across the ropes into a crowd when spectators are on the field. The provisions of Rule 7.04 c shall prevail as pertains to runners (f).

If a fielder, after catching a fly ball, falls into a bench making a catch, steps into a bench, but does not fall, the ball is in play and runners may advance at their own peril.

● When an umpire orders a player or any other person removed from the playing field (g).

● Except in the cases stated in paragraphs b and c (1) of this rule, no umpire shall call "Time" while play is in progress (h).

After the ball is dead, play is to be resumed when the pitcher takes his place on the pitcher's plate with a new ball or the same ball in his possession, and the plate umpire calls "Play." The plate umpire shall call "Play" as soon as the pitcher takes his place on his plate with the ball in his possession (5.11).

play

6.00 THE BATTER

THE BATTER—6.00

Batting Order (6.01)
● Each player of the offensive team shall bat in the order that his name appears in his team's batting order (a).
● After the first inning, the first batter in each inning shall be the player whose name follows that of the last player who legally completed his time of bat in the preceding inning (b).

Batter's Position in the Batter's Box (6.02)
● The batter shall take his position in the batter's box promptly when it is his time at bat (a).
● The batter shall not leave his position in the batter's box after the pitcher comes to a set position or starts his windup. If the batter does so, and the pitcher pitches, the umpire shall call "Ball" or "Strike," as the case may be.

Unless he requests the umpire to call "Time," the batter leaves the batter's box at the risk of having a strike delivered and called. The batter is not at liberty to step in and out of the batter's box at will.

Once a batter has taken his position in the batter's box, he shall not be permitted to step out of the batter's box in order to use the resin or the pine tar rag, unless there is a delay in the game action or, in the umpire's judgment, weather conditions warrant an exception.

Umpires are not to call "Time" at the request of the batter or any member of his team once the pitcher has started his windup or come to a set position, even though the batter claims, "dust in my eyes," "steamed glasses," "didn't get the sign," or for any other cause.

Umpires may grant a hitter's request for "Time" once he is in the batter's box, but the umpire should eliminate walking out of the batter's box without reason. If umpires are not lenient, batters will understand that they are in the batter's box and must remain there until the ball is pitched.

If a pitcher delays once the batter is in his box and the umpire feels that the delay is not justified, he may allow the batter to step out of the box momentarily.

If, after a pitcher starts his windup or comes to a set position with a runner on base, he does not go through with his pitch because the batter has stepped out of the box, it shall be called a balk. Both the pitcher and batter have violated a rule and the umpire shall call "Time," and both the batter and pitcher are to start over from "scratch" (b).
● If the batter refuses to take his position in the batter's box during his time at bat, the umpire shall order the pitcher to pitch and shall call "Strike" on each such pitch. The batter may take his proper position after each such pitch, and the regular ball and

strike count shall continue. But if the batter does not take his proper position before three strikes are called, he shall be declared out.

The batter's legal position shall be with both feet within the batter's box. The lines defining the batter's box are within the box (6.03).

A batter has legally completed his time at bat when he is put out or becomes a runner (6.04).

A batter is out when (6.05):
● His fair or foul fly ball (other than a foul tip) is legally caught by a fielder (a).
● A third strike is legally caught by the catcher. "Legally caught" means that the ball is in the catcher's glove before it touches the ground. It is not a legal catch if the ball lodges in the catcher's clothing or paraphernalia, or if it touches the umpire and is caught by the catcher on the rebound (b).
If a foul tip strikes the catcher's glove, goes on through to his chest protector, and he catches it with both hands against his body or protector, it is a strike. If it is a third strike, the batter is out. If the ball is smothered against the catcher's body or protector, it is a catch provided the ball struck the catcher's glove or hand first.
● A third strike is not caught by the catcher when first base is occupied before two are out (c).

62

- He bunts foul on a third strike (d).
- An infield fly is declared (e).
- He attempts to hit a third strike and the ball touches him (f).
- His fair ball touches him before touching a fielder (g).
- After hitting or bunting a fair ball, his bat hits the ball a second time in fair territory. The ball is dead and no runners may advance. If the batter-runner drops his bat and ball rolls against the bat in fair territory and, in the umpire's judgment, there was no intention to interfere with the course of the ball, the ball is alive and in play (h).

If a bat breaks, and part of it is in fair territory and is hit by a batted ball, or part of it hits a runner or fielder, play shall continue and no interference shall be called. If a batted ball hits part of a broken bat in foul territory, it is a foul ball.

If a whole bat is thrown into fair territory and interferes with a defensive attempting to make a play, interference shall be called, whether intentional or not.

In cases where a batting helmet is accidentally hit with a batted or thrown ball, the ball remains in play as if it had not hit the helmet.

If a batted ball strikes a batting helmet or any object foreign to the natural ground while in foul territory, it is a foul ball and the ball is dead.

If, in the umpire's judgment, there is intent on the part of the base runner to interfere with a batted or thrown ball by dropping the helmet or throwing it at the ball, the runner is out, the ball dead and runners must return to the last bases they legally touched.

- After hitting or bunting a foul ball, he intentionally deflects the course of the ball in any manner while running to first base. The ball is dead and the runners are to return to their original bases (i).
- After a third strike or after the batter hits a fair ball, either the batter or first base is tagged before the batter touches first base (j).
- In running the second half of the distance from home base to first base while the ball is being fielded to first base, the batter runs outside (to the right of) the three-foot lane, or inside (to the left of) the foul line, and in the umpire's judgment thereby interferes with the fielder taking the throw at first base. Of course, the batter is permitted to run outside the three-foot lane or inside the foul line to avoid colliding with a fielder attempting to field a batted ball (k).
- A fielder intentionally drops a fair fly ball or line drive with first, first and second, first and third, or first, second and third base occupied before two are out. The ball is dead and the runners must return to their original bases. In such a situation, the batter is not out if the fielder permits the ball to drop untouched to the ground, except when the infield fly-rule

63

applies (l).

• A preceding runner, in the umpire's judgment, intentionally interferes with a fielder's attempt to catch or throw a ball in his effort to complete a play (m).

• With two out and a count of two strikes on the batter, the runner on third base attempts to steal home base on a legal pitch, and the ball touches the runner in the batter's strike zone. The umpire calls "Strike three," the batter is out, and the run does not count. Should the umpire call "Strike three" before two are out, however, the ball is dead and the run counts (n).

A batter is out for illegal action when (6.06):

• He hits an illegally battted ball. If the batter hits a ball fair or foul while out of the batter's box, he is to be called out. Umpires shall pay particular attention to the position of the batter's feet if he attempts to hit the ball while he is being intentionally passed. A batter cannot jump or step out of the batter's box and hit the ball (a).

• He steps from one batter's box to the other while the pitcher is in a position ready to pitch (b).

• He interferes with the catcher's fielding or throwing by stepping out of the batter's box or making any other movement, that hinders the catcher's play at home plate. The batter is not to be declared out, however, should any runner who is attempting to advance is put out, or if a runner attempting to score is called out by reason of batter's interference.

If the batter interferes with the catcher, the plate umpire shall call "interference." The batter is out and the ball dead. No player may advance on such interference, and all runners must return to the last bases they had touched, in the umpire's judgment, at the time of the interference.

If, however, the catcher makes a play and a runner attempting to advance is out, it is to be assumed there was no actual interference; the runner is out, not the batter. Any other runners on the bases may advance. Play proceeds just as if no violation had been called.

If a batter strikes at a ball and misses, and swings so hard he carries the bat all the way around, and, in the umpire's judgment, unintentionally hits the catcher, or hits the ball in back of him on the backswing before the catcher has securely held the ball, it shall be called a strike. The ball is dead, however, and no runner shall advance on the play (c).

• He uses or attempts to use a bat that, in the umpire's judgment, has been altered or tampered with in such a way as to improve the bat's distance factor or cause an unusual reaction on the baseball. This includes bats that are filled, flat-surfaced, nailed, hollowed, grooved or covered with a substance such as paraffin, wax, etc. No advancement on the bases will be allowed, and any out or outs made during the play shall stand. In addition to being called out, the player is to be ejected from the game and may be subject to additional penalties as determined by the league president (d).

Batting out of Turn (6.07).

● A batter shall be called out—on appeal—when fails to bat in his proper turn, and another turn and another batter completes a time at bat in his place (a).

(1) The proper batter may take his place in the batter's box at any time before the improper batter becomes a runner or is put out, and any balls and strikes shall be counted in the proper batter's time at bat.

● When an improper batter becomes a runner or is put out, and the defensive team appeals to the umpire before the first pitch to the next batter of either team, or before any play or attempted play, the umpire (1) shall declare the proper batter to be out and (2) nullify any advance or score that may have occurred because of a ball batted by the improper batter, or because of his advance to first base through an error, base on balls, hit batter, or otherwise.

While the improper batter is at bat, if a runner advances on a stolen base, balk, wild pitch, or passed ball, such advance is legal (b).

● When an improper batter becomes a runner or is put out, and a pitch is made to the next batter of either team before an appeal is made, the improper batter thereby becomes the proper batter and the results of his time at bat become legal (c).

● When the proper batter is called out because he has failed to bat in turn, the next batter shall be the batter whose name follows that of the proper batter who was called out (d) (1).

When an improper batter becomes a proper batter because no appeal is made before the next pitch, the next batter shall be the batter whose name follows that of the legalized proper batter. The instant an improper batter's actions are legalized, the batting order picks up with the name following that of the legalized improper batter (d) (2).

The umpire is not to direct the attention of any person to the presence of an improper batter in the batter's box.

The batter becomes a runner
and is entitled to first base when (6.08):

● Four balls are called by the umpire (a).

A batter who is entitled to first base because of a base on balls must go to first base and touch the base before other base runners are forced to advance. This applies when the bases are full and when a substitute runner is put into the game.

If, in advancing, the base runner thinks there is a play and slides past the base before or after touching it, he may be put out by the fielder tagging him. If he fails to touch the base to which he is entitled, and attempts to advance beyond the base, he may be put out by a tag.

● He is touched by a pitched ball when he is not attempting to hit unless (b):

(1) The ball is in the strike zone when it touches the batter.

(2) The batter makes no attempt to avoid being touched by the ball.

If the ball is in the strike zone when it touches the batter, it shall be called a strike, whether or not the batter tries to avoid the ball. If the ball is outside the strike zone when it touches the batter, it shall be called a ball if he makes no attempt to avoid being touched.

● The catcher or fielder interferes with him. If a play follows the interference, the manager of the offense may advise the plate umpire that he elects to decline the interference penalty and accept the play. Such election must be made immediately at the end of the play. However, if the batter reaches first base on a hit, an error, a base on balls, a hit batsman, or otherwise, and all other runners advance at least one base, the play proceeds without

reference to the interference (c).

● A fair ball touches an umpire or a runner in fair territory before touching a fielder. If the fair ball touches an umpire after having passed a fielder other than the pitcher, or having touched a fielder, including the pitcher, the ball is in play (d).

The batter becomes a runner
when (6.09):

He hits a fair ball (a).

● The third strike called by the umpire is not caught (b), providing:

(1) First base is unoccupied.

(2) First base is occupied with two out.

When a batter becomes a base runner on a third-strike that is not caught by the catcher and then starts for the dugout or his position, and then realizes his situation and attempts to reach first base, he is not out unless he or first base is tagged before he reaches first base. If, however, he actually reaches the dugout or dugout steps, he may not attempt to then go to first base, and shall be out.

● A fair ball, after having passed a fielder other than the pitcher, or having been touched by a fielder including the pitcher, then touches an umpire or runner in fair territory (b).

66

safe!

• A fair fly ball that passes over a fence or into the stands after having traveled a distance of 250 feet or more from home plate. The batter is entitled to a home run, once he touches all the bases legally. A fair fly ball that passes out of the playing field, but travels less than 250 feet from home plate, entitles the batter to advance only as far as second base.

• A fair ball, after touching the ground, bounds into the stands; passes through, over, or under a fence; through, over, or under shrubbery or vines in the fence, or through or under a scoreboard. In any such case, the batter is entitled to a two-base hit and the runners advance two bases (e).

• A fair ball, before touching the ground, passes through or under a fence; through or under shrubbery or vines in the fence; through or under a scoreboard; through any opening in the fence or scoreboard, or which sticks in the fence or scoreboard. In any such case, the batter is entitled to a two-base hit and the runners are permitted to advance two bases (f).

• Any bounding ball in fair territory is deflected by a fielder into the stands or over or under a fence in either fair or foul territory. In either case, the batter is entitled to a two-base hit and any runners are permitted to advance two bases (g).

• Any fair fly ball is deflected by an infielder into the stands or over a fence into foul territory. In either case, the batter is entitled to a two-base hit. If, however, the ball is deflected into the stands or over a fence in fair territory, the batter is entitled to a home run, this is provided the point of deflection is at least 250 feet from home plate; otherwise, the batter is entitled to only a two-base hit (h).

Designated Hitter Rule (6.10).
• In the event of inter-league competition between clubs of leagues using the designated hitter rule and clubs of leagues not using the designated hitter rule,the rule is to be used as follows (a):
(1) In exhibition games, the rule will be used or not used as is the practice of the home team.
(2) In All Star games, the rule will only be used if both teams and both leagues so agree.
(3) In World Series play, the rule will be used every other year. It will not be used in 1977, it will be used in 1978, etc. (3).
• The rule provides as follows (b):
A hitter may be designated to bat for the starting pitcher and all subsequent pitchers in any game without otherwise affecting the status of the pitchers in the game. A designated hitter for a pitcher must be selected prior to the

game and his name must be included in the line-up cards presented to the umpire-in-chief.

It is not mandatory that a club designate a hitter for the pitcher, but failure to do so prior to the game precludes the use of a designated hitter for that game.

Pinch-hitters for the designated hitters may be used. Any substitute hitter for a designated hitter becomes the designated hitter. A replaced designated hitter is not permitted to re-enter the game in any capacity.

The designated hitter may be used defensively, continuing to bat in the same position in the batting order. The pitcher must then bat in the place of the substitute defensive player, unless more than one substitute is made. In such a case, the manager must designate their spots in the batting order.

A runner may be substituted for the designated hitter. The runner then assumes the role of the designated hitter. A designated hitter may not pinch run.

The role of the designated hitter is to be terminated for the remainder of the game should:
(1) The game pitcher be switched from the mound to a defensive position.
(2) A pinch hitter bats for any player in the batting order and then enters the game to pitch.
(3) The game pitcher bats for the designated hitter. (The game pitcher may only pinch-hit for the designated hitter.)
(4) A designated hitter assumes a defensive position in the field.

THE RUNNER—7.00

A runner acquires the right to an unoccupied base when he touches the base before he is out. He is then entitled to it until he is put out or forced to vacate it for another runner entitled to that base (7.01).

If a runner legally acquires title to a base, and the pitcher assumes his pitching position, the runner may not return to the previously occupied base.

In advancing, a runner shall touch first, second, third and home base in order. If forced to return, he shall retouch all the bases in reverse order, unless the ball is dead under the provisions of Rule 5.09. In such cases, the runner must go directly to his original base (7.02).

Two runners may not occupy a base. But if, while two runners are touching a base while the ball is alive, the following runner shall be out when tagged. The preceding runner is entitled to the base (7.03).

Each runner, other than the batter, may advance one base without any liability of being put out, when (7.04):

- There is a balk (a).
- The batter's advance, without liability (such as a base on ball), forces the runner to vacate his base (b).

A runner forced to advance without liability to be put out may advance past the base to which he is entitled, but only at his peril. If such a runner is put out for the third out of an inning before preceding runner touches home plate, the run shall score.

- A fielder, after catching a fly ball, falls into a bench or stand, or, when spectators are on the field, falls across ropes into the spectators (c).

A fielder or catcher may reach, step into or go into the dugout with one or both feet to make a catch and, if he holds the ball, the catch is allowed; the ball is in play.

If the fielder or catcher, after having made a legal catch, should fall into a stand or among spectators, or into the dugout, or fall while in the dugout, the ball is dead and runners advance one base without any liability to be put out.

- While he is attempting to steal a base, the batter is interfered with by the catcher or any other fielder (d).

Each runner, including the batter runner, may, without liability to be put out, advance (7.05):

- To home base, scoring a run, if a fair ball goes out of the playing field in flight, and he touches all the bases legally. Or if a fair ball which, in the umpire's judgment, would have gone out of the playing field in flight, is deflected by the act of a fielder in throwing his glove, cap, or any article of his apparel (a).

- Three bases, if a fielder deliberately touches a fair ball with his cap, mask or any part of his uniform detached from its proper place on his person. The ball remains in play and the batter can advance to home base, but at his peril (b).

- Three bases, if a fielder deliberately throws his glove at and touches a fair ball. The ball is in play and the batter may advance to home base, but at his peril (c).

- Two bases, if a fielder deliberately touches a thrown ball with his cap, mask or any part of his uniform detached from its proper place on his person. The ball remains in play (d).

- Two bases, when a fielder deliberately throws his glove at and touches a thrown ball. The ball is in play (e).

- Two bases, if a fair ball bounces or is deflected into the stands outside the first or third base foul lines; if it goes through or under a field fence; through or under a scoreboard; through or under shrubbery or vines on the fence, or if it becomes trapped in such a fence, scoreboard, shrubbery or vines (f).

- Two bases when, with no spectators on the playing field, a thrown ball goes into the stands, or bench, over, under or through a field fence, onto the slanted part of the screen above the backstop, or remains trapped in the mesh of a wire screen protecting the spectators.

In all such cases, the ball is dead. When a wild throw is the first play by an infielder, the umpire, in awarding the base advance, is to be governed by the position of the runners at the time the ball was pitched. In all other cases, the umpire shall be governed by the position of the runners at the time the wild throw was made (g).

● One base, if a ball that is pitched to the batter, or thrown by the pitcher from his position on the pitcher's plate to a base in an effort to catch a runner, goes into a stand or a bench or over or through a field fence or backstop. In any such case, the ball is declared dead (h).

● One base, if the batter becomes a runner on the count of ball four or strike three, when the pitch passes the catcher and lodges in the umpire's mask or other umpire paraphernalia (i).

If the batter becomes a runner on a wild pitch that entitles the runners to advance one base, the batter-runner shall be entitled to first base only.

Obstruction is the act of a fielder who, while not in possession of the ball and not in the act of fielding the ball, impedes the progress of any runner. When obstruction occurs, the umpire is to call or signal "Obstruction" (7.06).

● If a play is being made on an obstructed runner, or if the batter-runner is obstructed before he touches first base, the ball is dead and all runners are permitted to advance, without the liability of being put out, to the bases they would have reached, in the umpire's judgment, had there been no obstruction.

The obstructed runner shall be awarded at least one base beyond the base he last touched legally before the obstruction. Any preceding runners that are forced to advance by the award bases as the penalty for obstruction, shall advance without the liability of being put out (a).

When a play is being made on an obstructed runner, the umpire shall signal obstruction in the same manner that he calls "Time," with both hands overhead. The ball is immediately dead when the signal is given. However, should a thrown ball be in flight before the obstruction is called by the umpire, the runners are to be awarded such bases on wild throws as they would have been awarded had no obstruction occurred. On a play where a runner is trapped between second and third, and the runner is obstructed by the third baseman while the throw is in flight from the shortstop, and the throw goes into the dugout, the obstructed runner is to be awarded home base. Any other runners on base in this situation would be awarded two bases from the base each last legally touched before the obstruction was called.

● If no play is being made on the obstructed runner, the play shall proceed until no further action is possible. The umpire shall then call "Time" and impose such penalties, if any, that, in his judgment, will nullify the act of obstruction (b).

Under Rule 7.06 (b), when the ball is not dead on obstruction, and an obstructed runner advances beyond the base which, in the umpire's judgment, he would have been awarded because of being obstructed, he does so at his own peril and may be tagged out.

The catcher, when he does not have the ball in his possession, has no right to block the pathway of a runner attempting to score. The base line belongs to the runner. The catcher is permitted to be in the baseline only when he is fielding the ball or already has the ball in his hand.

In cases where there is a runner on third base who is trying to score by means of a squeeze play or a steal, and the catcher or any other fielder steps on or in front of home base without possession of the ball, or touches the batter or his bat, the pitcher is to be charged with a balk as a result of the catcher's interference. The batter is to be awarded first base and the ball is to be declared dead (7.07).

Any runner is out when (7.08):
● (1) He runs more than three feet away from a direct line between bases to avoid being tagged, unless the action is to avoid interference with a fielder who is fielding a batted ball, or (2), after touching first base, he leaves the baseline, obviously abandoning his effort to touch the next base (a).

Any runner who leaves the baseline after reaching first base to head for his dugout or his playing position in the field, believing there is no further play, may be declared out if the umpire judges the runner to be abandoning his efforts to run the bases. Even though an out is called, the ball remains in play as regards the other runners.

● He intentionally interferes with a thrown ball or hinders a fielder attempting to make a play on a batted ball (b).

A runner who is adjudged to have hindered a fielder who is attempting to make a play on a batted ball is out, whether or not it was intentional. If, however, the runner has contact with a legally occupied base when he hinders the fielder, he shall not be called out unless, in the umpire's judgment, such hindrance, whether occurring in fair or foul territory, is deemed intentional. If the umpire declares the hindrance intentional, the following penalty applies: With less than two out, the umpire shall declare both the runner and batter out. With two out, the umpire shall declare the batter out.

Where there is a run-down play between third base and home plate, and the succeeding runner has advanced and is standing on third base when the runner in the run-down is called out for offensive interference, the umpire shall send the runner standing on third base back to second base. The same principle applies if there is a run-down between second and third base and the succeeding runner has reached second base.

● He is tagged while off his base when the ball is alive. However, a batter-runner cannot be tagged out after overrunning or oversliding first base if he returns to the base immediately (c).

(1) If the impact of the runner breaks a base loose from its position, no play can be made on that runner at that base if he has reached the base safely.

(2) If a base is dislodged from its position during a play, any following runner on the same play shall be considered as touching or occupying the base if, in the umpire's judgment, he is touching or occupying the point marked by the dislodged bag.

● He fails to retouch the base after a fair or foul ball is legally caught before he or his base is tagged by a fielder. (This is an appeal play. The runner is not to be called out for his failure to retouch his base after the first following pitch, or any play or attempted play) (d).

Runners need not "tag up" on a foul tip. They may steal on a foul tip. If a so-called tip is not caught, it becomes an ordinary foul. Runners then return to their bases.

● After he has been forced to advance by reason of the batter becoming a base runner, he fails to reach the next base before a fielder tags him or the base. If, however, a following runner is put out on a force play, the force is removed and the runner must be tagged to be put out. The force is removed as soon as the runner touches the base to which he is forced to advance. If he overslides or overruns the base, he must be tagged to be put out. If the forced runner, after touching the next base, retreats for any reason toward the base he last occupied, the force play is reinstated, and he again can be put out if a fielder tags the base to which he is forced (e).

● He is touched by a fair ball in fair territory before the ball has touched or passed an infielder. The ball is dead; no runner may advance, except any runner who is forced to advance. An exception occurs when a runner is touching his base when touched by an infield fly. The batter is out, not the runner. But if the runner is touched by an infield fly when

he is not touching his base, both he and the batter are out (f).
- He attempts to score on a play in which the batter interferes with the play at home base before two are out. With two out, the interference puts the batter out and no run is registered (g).
- He passes a preceding runner before the runner has been put out (h).
- After he has acquired legal possession of a base, he runs the bases in reverse order for the purpose of confusing the defense or making a travesty of the game. The umpire is to immediately call "Time" and declare the runner out (i).

If a runner touches an unoccupied base and then, thinking the ball was caught or being decoyed into returning to the base he last touched, he may be put out while returning to that base. But if he reaches the base safely, he cannot be put out while in contact with the base.

- He fails to return at once to first base after overrunning or oversliding it. If he attempts to run to second after overrunning or oversliding first, he is out when tagged. If he starts toward the bench or toward his position in the outfield after overrunning or oversliding, failing to return to first base at once, he is out—on appeal —when either he or first base is tagged (j).

The runner who touches first

base and then overruns it, and is declared safe by the umpire within the intent of Rule 4.09 (a), has "reached first base," and any run which scores on such a play counts, even though the runner subsequently becomes the third out for failure to return "at once," as covered in Rule 7.08 (j).

- In running or sliding for home base, he fails to touch home base and makes no attempt to return to the base. He is out—on appeal —when a fielder holds the ball in his hand and touches home base (k).

This rule applies only when a runner is on his way to the bench and the catcher is required to chase him. It does not apply in ordinary play where the runner misses the plate and then immediately makes an effort to touch the plate before being tagged. In this case, the runner must be tagged.

It is interference by a batter or runner when (7.09):
- After a third strike, he hinders the catcher in his attempt to field the ball (a).
- After hitting or bunting a fair ball, his bat hits the ball a second time in fair territory. The ball is declared dead and runners are not permitted to advance. However, if the batter-runner drops his bat and the ball rolls against the bat in fair territory, but, in the umpire's judgment, there was no intention

to interfere with the course of the ball, the ball is to be considered live and in play (b).

• He intentionally deflects the course of a foul ball in any manner (c).

• With less than two outs and a runner on third base, the batter hinders a fielder in making a play at home base, the runner is declared out as a result of the batter's interference (d).

• When one or more members of the offensive team stand around any base to which a runner is advancing in an attempt to confuse, hinder, or add to the difficulty of the fielders, the runner is to be declared out because of the interference of his teammates (e).

• When a batter or runner who has just been put out hinders or impedes an ensuing play being made on a runner, the runner shall be declared out because of his teammate's interference (f).

If a batter or runner continues to advance after he has been put out, he shall not, by virtue of that act alone, be considered as confusing, hindering or impeding the fielders.

• When, in the judgment of the umpire, a base runner, with the obvious intention of breaking up a double play, willfully and deliberately interferes with a batted ball, or interferes with a fielder in the act of fielding a batted ball, the ball is declared dead. The runner is called out for interfer-

ence. The batter-runner may also be called out as a result of the action of his teammates. In no event are runners permitted to advance or can runs be scored as a result of such action by a runner (g).

• When, in the judgment of the umpire, a batter-runner, with the obvious intention of attempting to break up a double play, willfullly or deliberately interferes with a batted ball, or interferes with a fielder in the act of fielding a batted ball, the ball is declared dead. The batter-runner is called out for interference. The runner who advanced to a point nearest to home plate is also called out. In no event shall runners be permitted to advance as a result of such interference (h).

• When, in the judgment of the umpire, the third-base or first-base coach, by touching or holding the runner, physically assists him in returning or leaving third base or first base (i).

• When, with a runner on third base, the base coach leaves his box and acts in such a manner as to draw a throw by a fielder (j).

• When, in running the second half of the distance from home base to first base while the ball is being fielded to first base, the runner runs outside of (to the right of) the three-foot lane, or inside (to the left of) the foul line and, in the umpire's judgment, interferes with the fielder taking the throw at first base or attempting to field a batted ball (k).

The lines marking the three-foot lane are part of that "lane," but the interpretation to be made is that a runner is required to have both feet within the three-foot "lane" or on the lines marking the "lane."

● When he fails to avoid a fielder who is attempting to field a batted ball or intentionally interferes with a thrown ball. If two or more fielders attempt to field a batted ball, and the runner comes in contact with one or more of them, the umpire shall determine which fielder is entitled to the benefit of this rule. He shall not declare the runner out for coming in contact with a fielder other than the one adjudged to be determined to be entitled to field the ball (l).

● When a fair ball goes through the infield, or goes by an infielder and touches a runner immediately in back of him, or touches a runner after being deflected by a fielder, the umpire shall not declare the runner out for being touched by a batted ball. In making such a decision, the umpire must be convinced that the ball passed through or by the infielder, and that no other infielder had a chance to make a play on the ball. If in the umpire's judgment, the runner deliberately and intentionally kicked the batted ball on which the infielder has missed a play, the runner shall be called out for interfer-

ence (m).

PENALTY FOR INTERFERENCE

The runner is out and the ball dead.

Any runner shall be called out —on appeal—when (7.10):

● After a fly ball is caught, he fails to touch his original base before he or the original base is tagged (a).

"Retouch" means to tag up and start by being in contact with the base after the ball is caught. A runner is not permitted to take a flying start from a position in back of the base.

● While advancing or returning to a base with the ball in play, the runner fails to touch each base in order before he or one of the missed bases is tagged (b).

(1) The runner is not permitted to return and touch a missed base after a following runner has scored.

(2) When the ball has been declared dead, the runner is not permitted to return to touch a missed base or one he has left after he has advanced to and touched a base beyond the missed base.

● He overruns or overslides first base and fails to return to the base immediately, and he or the base is tagged (c).

● He fails to touch home base and makes no attempt to return to that base, and home base is tagged (d).

Any appeal made under this rule must be made before the next pitch or before the next play or any attempted play. If the violation occurs during a play which ends a half inning, the appeal must be made before the defensive team leaves the field. Any appeal is not to be interpreted as a play or an attempted play. Successive appeals may not be made upon a runner at the same base. If the defensive team in its first appeal errs, a request for a second appeal on the same runner at the same base shall not be allowed by the umpire. For example, if the pitcher throws to first base to appeal and throws the ball into the stands, no second appeal would be permitted.

Note: Appeal plays may require an umpire to recognize an apparent "fourth out." If the third out is made during a play in which an appeal play is sustained on another runner, the appeal decision takes precedence in determining the out. If there is more than one appeal during a play that ends a half-inning, the defense may elect to take the out that gives it the advantage. For the purposes of this rule, the defensive team has "left the field" when the pitcher and all infielders have left fair territory on their way to the bench or clubhouse.

If two runners arrive at home plate at about the same time, and the first runner misses home plate but a second runner legally touches the plate, the first runner will be called out on appeal. If there are two outs and the first runner is tagged out on his attempt to come back and touch the base, or, on appeal, is called out, then he shall be considered as having been put out before the second runner scored; he becomes the third out. The second runner's run shall not count (as provided in Rule 7.12).

An appeal must be clearly intended to be an appeal, either by a verbal request or by a play or an act that unmistakably indicated an appeal to the umpire. It would not be an appeal for a player to inadvertently step on the base with a ball in his hand. Time is not out when an appeal is being made. If a pitcher balks when making an appeal, the balk shall be regarded as a play.

The players, coaches or any member of the offensive team are to vacate any space (including both dugouts) needed by a fielder who is attempting to field a batted or thrown ball. In any violation of this rule, interference shall be called and the batter or runner on whom the play is being made shall be called out (7.11)

Unless two are out, the status of a following runner is not affected by a preceding runner's failure to

touch or retouch a base. If, upon appeal, the preceding runner is the third out, no runners following him shall score. If such a third out is the result of a force play, neither preceding nor following runners shall score (7.12).

80

safe!

rule 8.02
(see page 86)

82

8.00 THE PITCHER

Legal pitching delivery. There are two legal pitching positions, the windup position and the set position. Either position may be used at either time (8.01).

The pitcher is to take his sign from the catcher while standing on the rubber. The pitcher may disengage the rubber after taking his sign, but may not step quickly onto the rubber and pitch. This may be judged a quick pitch by the umpire. When the pitcher disengages the rubber, he must drop his hands to his sides. A pitcher is not allowed to disengage the rubber after taking each sign.

● The Windup Position. The pitcher shall stand facing the batter, his entire pivot foot on, or in front of, and touching, but not off the end of the pitcher's plate, and the other foot free. From this position, any natural movement associated with his delivery of the ball to the batter commits him to pitch without interruption or alteration. He shall not raise either foot from the ground, except that in his actual delivery of the ball to the batter he may take one step backward and one step forward with his free foot.

When a pitcher holds the ball with both hands in front of his body, with his entire pivot foot on, or in front of and touching, but not off the end of the pitcher's

83

plate, and his other foot free, he will be considered in a windup position.

The pitcher may have one foot, but not the pivot foot, off the rubber, and any distance he may desire in back of a line that is an extension of the back edge of the pitcher's plate, but not at either side of the pitcher's plate.

With his free foot, the pitcher may take one step backward and one step forward, but under no circumstances to either side, that is, to either the first-base or third-base side of the pitcher's rubber.

From the windup position, the pitcher may:

(1) Deliver the ball to the batter.
(2) Step and throw to a base in an attempt to pick-off a runner.
(3) Disengage the rubber (in which case, he must drop his arms to his sides).

He is not permitted to go into a set or stretch position. If he does so, it is a balk.

● The Set Position. The set position shall be indicated by the pitcher when he stands facing the batter with his entire pivot foot on or in front of, and in contact with, and not off the end of the pitcher's plate. His other foot is in front of the pitcher's plate. He is holding the ball in both hands in front of his body, and comes to a complete stop.

From this set position, the pitcher may deliver the ball to the batter, throw to a base, or step back-

ward off the pitcher's plate with his pivot foot.

Before assuming a set position, the pitcher may elect to make any natural preliminary motion, such as that known as the "the stretch." But if he so elects, he shall come to a set position before delivering the ball to the batter.

After assuming the set position, any natural motion associated with his delivery of the ball to the batter commits him to pitch without alteration or interruption (b).

Preparatory to coming to a set position, the pitcher shall have one hand on his side. From this position, he shall go into his set position, as defined in Rule 8.01 (b), without interruption and in one continuous motion.

The whole width of the foot in contact with the rubber must be on the rubber. A pitcher cannot pitch from off of the end of the rubber, with just one side of his foot touching the rubber.

The pitcher, following his stretch, must (a) hold the ball in both hands in front of his body and come to a complete stop. This rule must be enforced. Umpires should watch closely; pitchers are constantly attempting to "beat the rule" in their efforts to hold runners on bases.

In cases where the pitcher fails to make the complete "stop" called for in the rules, the umpire should immediately call a "Balk."

● At anytime during the pitcher's preliminary movements and

until his natural pitching motion commits him to pitch, the pitcher may throw to any base, provided he steps directly toward the base before making the throw (c).

The pitcher must step "ahead of the throw." A snap throw followed by a step directly to the base is a balk.

● If the pitcher makes an illegal pitch with the bases unoccupied, the pitch shall be called a ball, unless the batter reaches first base on a hit, an error, a base on balls, hit batter, or otherwise (d).

A ball which slips out of the pitcher's hand and crosses the foul line shall be called a ball; otherwise, it will be called no pitch. It would be a balk with men on base.

● If the pitcher removes his pivot foot from contact with the pitcher's plate by stepping backward with that foot, he thereby becomes an infielder. If he then makes a wild throw from that position, it shall be considered a wild throw the same as a wild throw by any other infielder (e).

While off the rubber, the pitcher may throw to any base. If he makes a wild throw, the throw is a throw of an infielder and what follows is governed by the rules covering a ball thrown by a fielder.

The pitcher shall not (8.02):
(1) Bring his pitching hand in contact with his mouth or lips while in the 18-foot circle surrounding

the pitching rubber (a).

For violation of this part of the rule, the umpires shall immediately call a ball. If the pitch is made, however, and a batter reaches first base on a hit, an error, a hit batsman or otherwise, and no other runner is put out before advancing at least one base, the play shall proceed without reference to the violation. Repeated offenders shall be subject to a fine by the league president.

(2) Apply a foreign substance of any kind to the ball.

(3) Expectorate on the ball, either hand, or his glove.

(4) Rub the ball on his glove, person or clothing.

(5) Deface the ball in any manner.

(6) Deliver what is called a "shine" ball, "spit" ball, "mud" ball or "emery" ball. The pitcher, of course, is allowed to rub the ball between his bare hands.

For violation of any part of this rule, the umpire shall:

Call the pitch a ball, warn the pitcher and have announced on the public address system the reason for the action (A).

In the case of a second offense by the same pitcher in the same game, the pitcher shall be disqualified from the game (B).

If a play follows the violation called by the umpire, the manager of the offense may advise the umpire that he elects to accept the play. Such election shall be made immediately at the end of the play. However, if the batter

87

reaches first base on a hit, an error, a base on balls, a hit batsman, or otherwise, and no other runner is put out before advancing at least one base, the play shall proceed without reference to the violation (C).

Even though the offense elects to take the play, the violation shall be recognized and the penalties cited in (A) and (B) shall still be in effect (D).

The umpire shall be the sole judge as to whether any portion of this rule has been violated (E).

All umpires are to carry with them one official rosin bag. The umpire-in-chief is responsible for placing the rosin bag on the ground in back of the pitcher's plate. If the ball hits the rosin bag at any time, the ball is in play.

In the case of rain or a wet field, the umpire may instruct the pitcher to carry the rosin bag in his hip pocket. A pitcher may use the rosin bag for the purpose of applying rosin to his bare hand or hands. Neither the pitcher nor any other player shall dust the ball with the rosin bag. Neither the pitcher nor any other player is permitted to apply rosin from the bag to his glove, or dust any part of his uniform with the rosin bag.

● Have on his person or in his possession any foreign substance (b).

● When the batter is in position, intentionally delay the game by throwing the ball to players other than the catcher, except in an attempt to retire a runner.

If, after a warning by the umpire, such delaying action is repeated, the pitcher shall be removed from the game.

● Intentionally pitch at the batter (d).

If, in the umpire's judgment, such a violation occurs, the umpire shall warn the pitcher and his manager that another such pitch will mean the immediate expulsion of the pitcher. At the same time, the umpire shall warn the opposing manager that such an infraction by his pitcher shall result in the pitcher's expulsion.

If, in the umpire's judgment, there is another such pitch during the game by any pitcher, the umpire shall eject the pitcher from the game.

If, in the umpire's judgment, circumstances warrant, one or both teams may be officially "warned" prior to the game or in the case of an actual violation during the game in progress.

When a pitcher takes his position at the beginning of each inning, or when he relieves another pitcher, he shall be permitted to make not more than eight preparatory pitches to his catcher, during which time play shall be suspended. A league may limit the number of preparatory pitches to fewer than eight. Such preparatory pitches shall not consume more than one minute of time. If a sudden emergency causes a pitcher to be summoned into the game without the opportunity to warm up, the umpire-in-chief shall allow him as many pitches as the umpire deems necessary (8.03).

When the bases are unoccupied, the pitcher shall deliver the ball to the batter within 20 seconds after he receives the ball. Each time the pitcher delays the game by violating this rule, the umpire shall call a "Ball."

The intent of this rule is to avoid unnecessary delays. The umpire shall insist that the catcher return the ball promptly to the pitcher, and that the pitcher take his position on the rubber promptly. Obvious delay by the pitcher should be instantly penalized by the umpire (8.04).

If there is a runner or runners on the bases, it is a balk when (8.05):
● The pitcher, while touching his plate, makes any motion naturally associated with his pitch, and then fails to make such delivery (a).

If a pitcher swings his free foot past the back edge of the pitcher's rubber, he is required to pitch to the batter, except in cases where he throws to second base on a pick-off play.
● The pitcher, while touching his plate, feints a throw to first base and fails to complete the throw (b).

● The pitcher, while touching his plate, fails to step directly toward a base before throwing to that base (c).

If a pitcher turns or spins off his free foot without actually stepping, or if he turns his body and throws before stepping, it is a balk.

A pitcher must step directly toward a base before throwing to that base, but only in the case of first base is he then required to throw to that base. With runners on first and third, it is legal for the pitcher to step toward third and not throw, merely to bluff the runner back to third; then, seeing the runner on first base start for second, turn, step toward first base and throw to first. However, if with runners on first and third, the pitcher, while in contact with the rubber, steps toward third, and then immediately and in practically the same motion, "wheels" and throws to first base, it is obviously an attempt to deceive the runner at first base, and such a move shall be called a balk. Of course, if the pitcher steps off the rubber and then makes such a move, it is not a balk.
● The pitcher, while touching his plate, throws or feints a throw to an unoccupied base, except for the purpose of making a play (d).
● The pitcher makes an illegal pitch (e).

A quick pitch is an illegal pitch. Umpires will judge a quick pitch as one delivered before the batter is reasonably set in the batter's box. With runners on base, the penalty is a balk. With no runners on base, it is a ball. The quick pitch is dangerous and should not be permitted.

- The pitcher delivers the ball to the batter while he is not facing the batter (f).
- The pitcher makes any motion naturally associated with his pitch while he is not touching the pitcher's plate (g).
- The pitcher unnecessarily delays the game (h).
- The pitcher, without having the ball, stands on or astride the pitcher's plate, or, while off the plate, feints a pitch (i).
- The pitcher, after coming to a legal pitching position, removes one hand from the ball other than in actually pitching or in throwing to a base (j).
- The pitcher, while touching his plate, accidentally or intentionally drops the ball (k).
- The pitcher, while giving an intentional base on balls, pitches while the catcher is not in the catcher's box (l).
- The pitcher delivers the pitch from a set position without coming to a stop (m).

In each of these cases, the ball is dead and each runner advances one base without liability of being put out, unless the batter reaches first base on a hit, an error, a base on balls, hit batter, or otherwise. In any such case, all runners advance at least one base and play proceeds without reference to the balk.

A professional league shall adopt the following rule pertaining to the visit of the manager or coach to the pitcher (8.06):

- The rule limits the number of trips a manager or coach may make to any one pitcher in any one inning (a).
- A second trip to the same pitcher in the same inning will cause the pitcher's automatic removal (b).
- The manager or coach is prohibited from making a second visit to the mound while the same batter is at bat (c).
- If a pinch hitter is substituted for the batter, the manager or coach may make a second visit to the mound, but he must remove the pitcher.

A manager or coach is considered to have concluded his visit to the mound when he leaves the 18-foot circle surrounding the pitcher's rubber.

If the manager or coach goes to the catcher or an infielder, and that player then visits the pitcher, it is to be considered the same as the coach manager or a coach having visited the pitcher.

If a coach goes to the mound and removes a pitcher, and then the manager goes to the mound to talk to the new pitcher, it constitutes one trip to that pitcher that inning.

In a case where a manager has made his first trip to the mound and then returns to the mound a second time in the same inning with the same pitcher in the game and the same batter at bat, and having been warned by the umpire that he cannot return to the mound, the manager shall be removed from the game. The pitcher shall be required to pitch to the batter until he is retired or gets on base. After the batter is retired or becomes a base runner, the pitcher must be removed from the game. The manager should be notified that his pitcher is to be removed from the game after he pitches to one hitter, so he can have a substitute pitcher warmed up.

pitcher's motion to first base

you're out!

THE UMPIRE—9.00

The umpire is the official responsible for the conduct of the game, determining the fitness of the playing conditions, indicating when time is out, when the ball is in play, calling balls and strikes, indicating foul balls, calling whether a runner is out or safe at base, and deciding on any interpretations of the rules.

● The league president shall appoint one or more umpires to officiate at each league championship game. The umpires shall be responsible for the conduct of the game in accordance with these official rules and for maintaining discipline and order on the playing field during the game (9.01) (a).

● Each umpire is the representative of the league and of professional baseball, and is authorized and required to enforce all of these rules. Each umpire has the authority to order a player, coach, manager, club officer or employee to do or refrain from doing anything which affects the administering of these rules and enforcing the prescribed penalties (b).

● Each umpire has the authority to rule on any point not specifically covered in these rules (c).

● Each umpire has the authority to disqualify any player, coach, manager or substitute for objecting to decisions or for unsportsmanlike conduct or language, and to eject each disqualified person from the playing field. If an umpire disqualifies a player while a play is in progress, the disqualification is not to take effect until no further action is possible in that play (d).

• Each umpire has the authority to eject from the playing field any person whose duties permit his presence in the field, such as ground crew members, ushers, photographers, newsmen, broadcasting crew members, etc., and any spectator or other person not authorized to be on the playing field (e).

• **Any umpire's decision** that involves judgment is final. Such decisions can include, but are not limited to, whether a batted ball is fair or foul, whether a pitch is a strike or a ball, or whether a runner is safe or out. No player, manager, coach or substitute is permitted to object to any such judgment decisions.

Players are not permitted to leave their positions on the field or on base, nor are managers or coaches permitted to leave the bench or coach a coach's box to argue balls and strikes. A person starting for the plate to protest the call should be warned. If he continues toward the plate, he should be ejected from the game (9.02) (a).

• If there is a reasonable doubt that any umpire's decision may be in conflict with the rules, the manager may appeal the decision and ask that a correct ruling be made. Such an appeal is to be directed only to the umpire who made the protested decision (b).

• If a decision is appealed, the umpire making the decision may ask another umpire for information before announcing his final decision. No umpire shall criticize, seek to reverse or interfere with another umpire's decision, unless asked to do so by the umpire making it.

The manager or catcher may request the plate umpire to ask his partner for help on a half swing when the plate umpire calls the pitch a ball, but not when the pitch is called a strike. The manager may not complain that the umpire made an improper call, but only that he did not ask his partner for help. Field umpires must be alerted to the request from the plate umpire and quickly respond. Managers are not permitted to protest the call of a ball or strike on the pretense they are asking for information about a half swing.

Appeals on a half swing may be made only on the call of a ball. When asked to appeal, the home-plate umpire must refer to a base umpire for his judgment on the half swing. Should the base umpire call the pitch a strike, the strike shall prevail.

Base runners must be alerted that the plate umpire may reverse the call of a ball to one of a strike on an appeal from the plate umpire. In such a case, the runner is in jeopardy of being put out by the catcher's throw. Also, in a base-stealing situation, the catcher must be alert if a ball call is reversed to a strike call by the base umpire upon appeal from the plate umpire. On appeal in a half swing situation, the ball is considered to be in play.

If the manager leaves the dugout or a coach's box to argue with the first or third base umpire on a half swing, and after being warned he persists in arguing, he can be ejected (since he is arguing over a called ball or strike) (c).

● No umpire may be replaced during a game unless he is injured or becomes ill (d).

If there is only one umpire, he shall have complete jurisdiction in administering the rules. He may take any position on the playing field which will enable him to discharge his duties (usually behind the catcher, but sometimes behind the pitcher if there are runners) (9.03) (a).

If there are two or more umpires, one shall be designated umpire-in-chief and the others field umpires (b).

The umpire-in-chief, usually called the plate umpire, shall stand behind the catcher. His duties are to (9.04):

(1) Take full charge of and be responsible for the proper conduct of the game.
(2) Call and keep count of the balls and strikes.
(3) Call and declare fair balls and fouls, except those commonly called by the field umpires.
(4) Make all decisions on the batter.
(5) Make all decisions except those commonly reserved for the field umpires.
(6) Decide when a game shall be forfeited.
(7) If a time limit has been set, announce that fact and the time-limit set before the game starts.
(8) Inform the official scorer of the batting order, and, upon request, any changes in the line-up or batting order.
(9) Announce, at his discretion, any special ground rules.

● A field umpire may take any position on the playing field he thinks best suited to make impending decisions on the bases. His duties are to (b):
(1) Make all decisions on the bases except those that are specifically reserved for the umpire-in-chief.
(2) Take concurrent jurisdiction with the umpire-in-chief in calling "Time", balks, illegal pitches, or the defacement or discoloration of the ball by any player.
(3) Aid the umpire-in-chief in every manner enforcing the rules. Except in his power to forfeit the game, the plate umpire

shall have equal authority with the umpire-in-chief in administering and enforcing the rules and maintaining discipline.

● If different decisions should be made on one play by different umpires, the umpire-in-chief shall call the umpires into consultation with no manager present. After such consultation, the umpire-in-chief (unless another umpire has been designated by the league president) is to determine which decision shall prevail, based on which umpire was in the best position to see the play and which decision was most likely to be correct. Play shall then proceed as if only the final decision had been made (c).

● Within twelve hours after the end of a game, the umpire shall report to the league president all violations of the rules and other incidents worthy of comment, including the disqualification of any trainer, manager, coach or player, and the reasons therefore (9.05) (a).

● When any trainer, manager, coach or player is disqualified for a flagrant offense, such as the use of obscene or indecent language, or an assault upon an umpire, trainer, manager, coach or player, the umpire shall forward full particulars to the league president within four hours after the end of the game (b).

● After receiving the umpire's report that a trainer, manager, coach, or player has been dis-

qualified, the league president shall impose such a penalty as he deems justified, and shall then notify the person penalized and the manager of the club of which the penalized person is a member. If the penalty includes a fine, the penalized person shall pay the amount of the fine to the league within five days after receiving notice of the fine. Failure to pay such a fine within the five-day period shall result in the offender being barred from participation in any game and from sitting on the players' bench during any game, until the fine is paid (c).